# The Great European Schools of Classical Dressage

## Vienna
## Saumur
## Jerez
## Lisbon

Alain Laurioux
Guillaume Henry

CADMOS

# Acknowledgements

The authors would particularly like to thank Jean-Claude Barry, Graham Bushnell, Magali Clique, General Dupuy de La Grand'Rive, Line Le Bras, General Pierre Durand, Jean-Louis Gouraud, Kathy Reymann, Frédérique Said, Marisol Sánchez, Antoine Sinniger, Catherine Thominet, Anne Vignau and Georgina Whittle for their help.

As well as Elisabeth Gürtler and Ernst Bachinger, Jacques Thiolat and Colonel Jean-Michel Faure, Francisco Manuel Reina Osuna and Manuel Ruiz Gutierrez and Doctor Filipe Figueiredo Graciosa.

Original edition : Les hauts lieux de l'art équestre © Éditions Belin – Paris, 2008
Copyright of this edition © 2009 by Cadmos Books, Great Britain
Conception and Design : Rampazzo & Associés
Translated into English by Chloë Jacquet, Equivalence Ltd – Equestrian Translation
Editorial of the English edition: Linda Robinson, Christopher Long
British Library Cataloguing in Publication Data

A catalogue record of this book is available from the British Library.

Printed in Germany

ISBN 978-3-86127-968-6

# Contents

# Prefaces, after Paris-Bercy (November 2007)

# The Spanish Riding School in Vienna

The Spanish Riding School in Vienna is one of Austria's major cultural treasures and the oldest equestrian institution in the world. For over four centuries, the authentic classical doctrine of equestrian art's Haute École has been preserved there.

Our first, and most noble duty, remains the training of our inestimable horses, the Lipizzaners, whilst maintaining the traditions of ancient masters such as La Guérinière and Pluvinel. However we are equally responsible for transmitting this art to younger generations in order to ensure the permanence of the institution. Also considering itself to be a cultural ambassador for Austria, the Spanish Riding School in Vienna takes great care of a living heritage, still preserved, for the whole world to get close to the beauty of classical dressage and to be encouraged to honour this tradition.

The Lipizzaners and the famous Winter Riding School, completed in 1735 by Josef Emanuel Fischer von Erlach, are inseparable. This jewel of baroque art, commissioned by Emperor Charles VI is, quite rightly, considered to be the most beautiful riding school in the world. Only the portrait of the Emperor on horseback provides a shimmering contrast to the elegance and sobriety of the arena, creating an atmosphere worthy of the practice of classical riding. Following the ancient masters' classical ideology, the horses' well-being is constantly put first. A slowly and carefully trained horse should, throughout its education, become more beautiful, calmer and more expressive. As Pluvinel correctly pointed out: let us be wary of upsetting a young horse, for his grace resembles the scent of a flower that, once evaporated, will never return.

Tradition is of utmost importance within "The Spanish", the affectionate nickname given to the school by the Viennese. This begins with the uniforms of the Empire which we put on daily for training and performances and ends with the carrying of the birch crop which symbolises modesty and humility when faced with Art. Those who have the opportunity to work in this institution are aware of the great privilege.

The joint performance in Paris in November 2007 with the great schools of France, Spain and Portugal, was a unique and extraordinary adventure for me. One which I would not have wished to be deprived of and the wonderful memory of which I will always cherish.

**Ernst Bachinger**
*Director of the Spanish Riding School in Vienna*

# The Cadre Noir in Saumur

In grouping the master riders of the four European schools within this book, the Spirit itself achieves the unification of the forces of equestrian art. This takes place in a unique way, a way that differentiates it from all other encounters. This is what constitutes its original usefulness and the particular need for it.

The week of Paris-Bercy 2007 allowed us to collaborate within a full dynamic of forward thinking and in an activity that has found its own aim: to awaken emotions thanks to the beauty of the classically trained horse, but also to promote the values of equestrianism that needed to be preserved and transcended.

All the difficulties were overcome as this meeting's actual aim was to conquer them: to achieve the union of the four schools. We now know the profound meaning that ran through this exchange.

These values, as demonstrated by the desire to perform together, can be found illustrated throughout the pages of this book. The homogeneity of the photographs taken by a single photographer, Alain Laurioux, is their living testimony. May this book be the driving force that allows for the perpetuation of the deep meaning of the story of our common heritage: "Equitation is the best foundation to the art of controlling oneself" (Montaigne).

**Colonel Jean-Michel Faure**
*Head rider of the Cadre Noir in Saumur*

# The Royal Andalusian School of Equestrian Art in Jerez

On behalf of the Real Escuela Andaluza del Arte Ecuestre, I would like to reassert the honour that it was for our Institution to participate in this historical equestrian ensemble with the Spanish School of Vienna, the Cadre Noir of Saumur and the Portuguese School of Equestrian Art at Bercy in November 2007. The master riders from all four schools, with their characteristics and their horses of different breeds, presented, in front of an enthusiastic audience, a show which demonstrated that the basis of our equestrianism, the Haute École, is the same for us all.

Vienna, Saumur, Lisbon and Jerez are towns that are historically linked to the horse. Thanks to meetings such as the one in Paris-Bercy in November 2007 we are contributing to the establishment of a uniting link between cultures, the roots of which are historically intertwined.

The Real Escuela Andaluza del Arte Ecuestre has managed to marry tradition with progress. Its main objectives are the conservation and dressage of the Spanish horse – noble and harmonious in its movements and with the same characteristics, since the fifteenth century, as the breed created by the Carthusian monks – the diffusion of equestrian art, the training of master riders, of elite sportspeople, of artisans of the horse world and to be an ambassador abroad for Andalusia and Spain.

We hope that new collaborations between the four schools will take place in the near future.

**Manuel Ruiz Gutiérrez**

*Head rider of the Royal Andalusian School of Equestrian Art in Jerez*

# The Portuguese School of Equestrian Art in Lisbon

The world's four great schools are assembled in this wonderful book: such beauty, such class, such richness in this global cultural heritage! This book is the outcome of a long and beautiful story, of a profound and serious art which more and more enthusiasts embrace each time throughout the world. Within these four institutions there are localised differences, in uniform, tack, music, choreography, horses and even some different exercises! But, as we demonstrated to the audience in Bercy during the four schools' first appearance together in the same performance, a common sentiment and spirit exist: to work meticulously, with motivated and happy horses!

We have shown that, without competition, it is possible to collaborate and work together within the basic principles of academic equitation. The emphasis is placed on functionality and beauty, whilst making the most of the gaits and natural expression of the horses, working to the limits of artistic gymnastics and dance using each horse's unique characteristics whilst always respecting psychological and physical equilibrium.

The great atmosphere during rehearsals, the human and technical exchanges amongst almost sixty master riders and about a hundred horses present at this great show, have been an unforgettable experience for us all as well as for the general public that filled the hall for those three evenings of November 2007.

With Alain Laurioux's photographs, this book is an extraordinary document in the history of global Haute École.

**J. Filipe Figueiredo (Graciosa)**
*Director and head rider of the Portuguese School of Equestrian Art in Lisbon*

# Introduction

When classical equitation is mentioned, four names spring to mind: the Spanish Riding School in Vienna, the Cadre Noir in Saumur, the Portuguese School of Equestrian Art in Lisbon and the Royal Andalusian School of Equestrian Art in Jerez. Throughout the world, these four schools are considered to be the inheritors of an "equestrian tradition" in its most artistic, most accomplished and most noble form.

Beyond their common roots, they however have distinct histories and discrete equestrian doctrines. Moreover, the study and comparison of their respective aims, their functioning, their selection requirements – as much for riders as for horses – and of their own particular work methods, helps to reinforce that impression of unity and diversity that one gets at first glance. Furthermore, they enable us to grasp their originality, their contribution and, whilst understanding their past, to clarify their present and to give us a glimpse into their future at the heart of a developing Europe.

When Ferdinand the Catholic, by then King Ferdinand II of Aragon, decided, in 1494, to reconquer the kingdom of Naples and to drive the French out of "his" kingdom, he started a revolution that he probably did not even suspect: that of equestrian art.

Indeed, Ferdinand's army, under the supervision of "The Great Captain" Gonzalo Fernandez de Cordoba, was made up of foot soldiers and a majority of riders: the caballeria despuela dorada (the golden-spurred knights). This cavalry represented the mid-ranking nobility of the kingdom of Castile. They were mounted on horses that could be found on the Peninsula, and in particular Andalusian horses, also known as the Spanish jennet.

These unique horses have extraordinary natural abilities in terms of mobility, speed and attention. These qualities, which proved their worth many times against the Moors, are protected like treasure. The breed is carefully maintained and developed through selection and rigorous schooling. In fact, in the municipality of Jerez de la Frontera's archives, there is a decree from 1490 prohibiting the sale of foals without express authority from the *alcade* (the mayor).

The word "jennet" comes from the Spanish words *jinete*, rider, and *jineta*, which describes the short spear carried by the rider. The "Great Captain's" riders (the jennets) rode in a style known as "a la jineta". They were protected by light armour, wore boots and were armed with a *jineta* and a curved sabre. For a mouthpiece they used a Moorish bit with a rigid curb chain and two single reins.[1] The saddle's front and back (the battes) were quite low. Their stirrups were worn short and had a wide tread. Their legs therefore formed a Z shape, for their joints (hips, knees, ankles) were slightly bent. This gave them a certain mobility which allowed them to stand up in their saddle, to hit from above. They gained strength and flexibility and thus compensated for the relatively small size of their horses.

Previous page facing
Carousel of the riders
from the Viennese
School at Paris-Bercy
(November 2007).

Opposite
A Cadre Noir jumper
performing a terre-a
terre in preparation for
a capriole.

When these noblemen were not at war, they amused themselves playing games which also served as training. The most popular pastime was hunting or, better still, bullfighting. Tauromachy has always helped the Spanish and Portuguese keep their equestrian tradition alive. Initially the "entertainment" consisted of letting a bull loose on the square in the middle of the crowd (on foot). Amidst the screams, the bull charged randomly. At first everyone endeavoured to avoid it and then to repeatedly stab it until it died. Some spectators lost their lives to the game: those that were too slow, or those that were too foolhardy. However, with the horse (always) being a sign of social status, the noblemen proceeded differently (of course) to the lower-classed people: they faced the bull in a more confined space, reserved for specially handpicked participants. Even though, at the end of the fifteenth century, the short spear (the rejon) had not yet definitively replaced the lance and even though the caballero still wore armour, it had lightened considerably, and he battled and fought the bull up close. Therefore the horse's training was vital: it had to be flexible and capable of rapidly starting or stopping in response to the slightest indication from its rider. The "art" was subtle, dangerous but also striking, virile and admired. Indeed, neither Charles V (1500-58) nor his son Philippe II (1527-98) hesitated in facing danger and subjecting themselves to popular judgement by entering the arena, sometimes kill-ing on horseback with the rejon, sometimes on foot with a sword and using a cape as a lure.

The French, on the other hand, rode heavy and imposing horses, more akin to light draught horses (as were used in the fields) than to thoroughbreds (as seen on racetracks). They had to carry heavy armour (both theirs and their rider's), sizeable tack (especially the saddle), and the equitation was roughly the same as was practised in the Middle Ages. Even though these riders were beginning to develop their horses' responsiveness – since the advent of firearms on the battle field, it was no longer sufficient to charge but instead they had to move forward in a compact mass, stop, fire, then turn around to retreat at a gallop – the riding had hardly changed. The French kept to a double bridle and four reins. Their saddles were high at the front and back to keep the riders firmly wedged. The rider's upper body was held very upright, if not leaning slightly back, the stirrups worn very long, the legs almost straight. This style of seat was a left-over from a very recent past during which one of the favourite forms of entertainment – jousting – consisted of two riders launched at each other at a full gallop, with shields, lances and armour, trying to knock each other out of their saddles. The shock of these two masses of over seven hundred kilos (1500 pounds) (horse, rider and their armour) at speeds of between thirty and thirty-five kilometres per hour (19-22 miles per hour) (at a gallop) is equivalent to a jump from a third floor window! The Frenchmen's horses were only very roughly trained. They proceeded at walk or gallop, and once they had set off it was difficult to slow them down, let alone make them turn. But naturally, the impact on the enemy was formidable!

Opposite
The riders of the
Portuguese School
practising at their
facilities in Lisbon.

Therefore, in the late fifteenth century there were the Spanish on the one hand, with their riding "a la jineta", a fast, mobile style ideal for combat and, on the other, the French who, like the rest of Europe, rode in a more forward-going style, relying on the force and power of the impact. The Spanish proved to have the upper hand in this contest. Although the equitation being practised was not solely responsible for this, there is no doubt that it contributed to the victory of the one and the defeat of the other. These highly focussed "little" horses that stopped, turned, "flew" to the side or suddenly leapt forward with extreme ease, placed an extraordinary weapon at their riders' disposal: mobility in all directions.

The multi-faceted progress – cultural, artistic and scientific – that was already stirring in Italy, rapidly took on this challenge. Unable to get their mounts to achieve what they saw others do with ease, the Italians, rapidly followed by the French, sought to standardise practices, which would bring the same degree of ease to their horses as that observed in the Iberians'.

To get an idea of the difficulty of this task, it is important to know that, in the wild, horses are prey. To escape from their predators, they have to flee. Nature has therefore "designed" the horse to run fast, with long and low movements and bearing their weight on their shoulders, as seen on the racetrack. However exactly the opposite is required to gain mobility in all directions! The horse needs to gather itself, to collect its weight over its hindquarters, like a cat about to pounce and to be able to launch itself forwards, upwards or to the side. All of this, of course, in response to its rider's slightest instruction: the ability to fight and to survive depends upon it. It is indeed hard to imagine a soldier whose horse is bolting towards enemy lines and unable to stop, or one riding a horse that cannot (or will not) turn: it would mean certain death. It must therefore not only be able to turn, stop, start, but also to do it as soon as told to by its rider. To achieve this, not only for itself but also with the weight it is carrying, it must be trained, both physically and mentally, to be able to and to want to. The "science" of equitation was born. Through a methodical and in-depth study of cause and effect, it researched the mental and physical gymnastics which would allow non-Iberian horses to be handled by their riders with an impulsion and skill similar to that of the Spanish. In Italy, in France and then throughout the whole of Europe, thousands of men devoted their whole lives – sometimes in extreme poverty – seeking, fumbling, going astray and slowly finding the ins and outs of this ideal. Experimenting with all breeds and in all possible disciplines (riding at war, at court, in the circus, for sport etc), these men were both reflections of their period and links in a long chain which, even today, continues to develop its knowledge.

Above
A Lipizzaner in
training, performing a
pesade in Vienna.

Opposite
A School of Jerez
rider performing a
"Viennese" courbette.

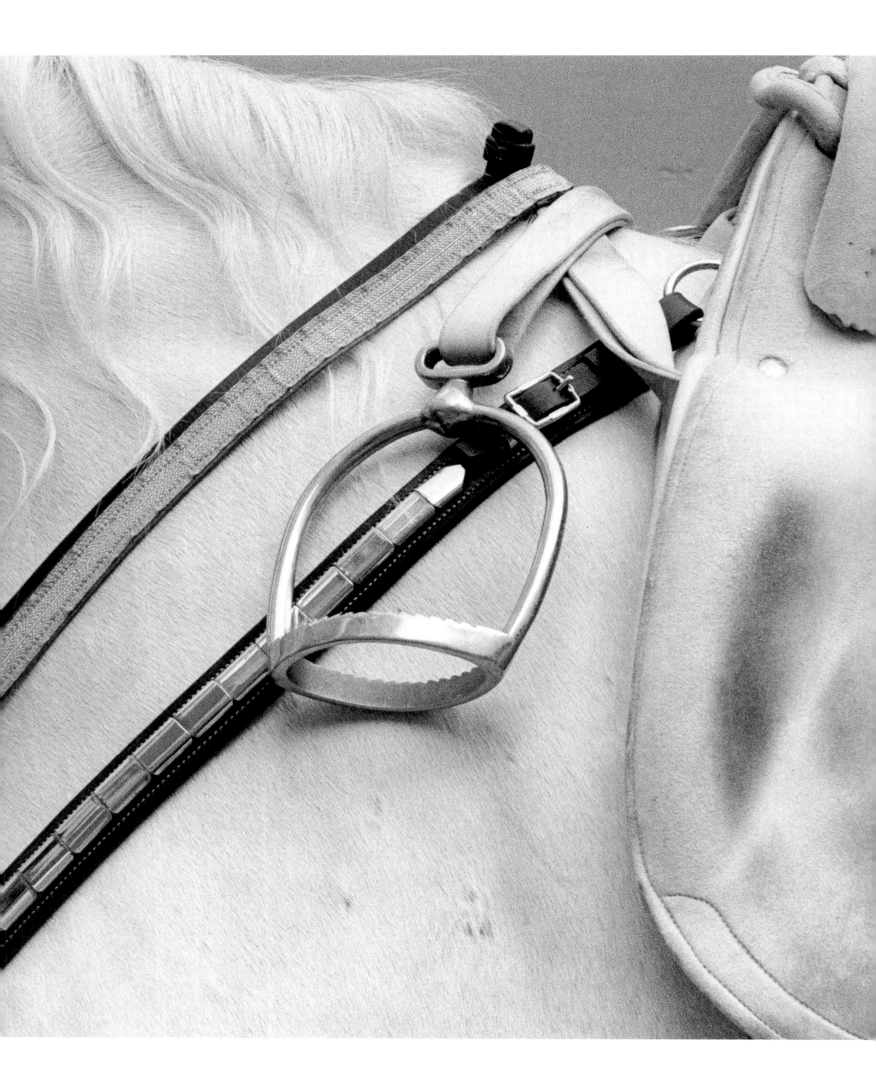

# From Grisone to La Guérinière

In France, one generally distinguishes between four great movements:
– the "ancient equitation", resulting from sixteenth century Italian riding, the peak of which was the School of Versailles in the eighteenth century. It was the king's equitation, for he who could control his horse could govern his people;
– the school of Auvergne, the original military equitation;
– the Baucher riding style which culminated in the "second manner" in the latter half of the nineteenth century;
– a second military type of riding, invented by the Comte d'Aure, which broke with the previous trends and marked the start of contemporary riding.

Here, the first trend is of particular interest as within it lies the origins of the schools of Vienna, Saumur, Lisbon and Jerez.

The "science" of equitation began in Italy. In 1532, a great equestrian academy saw the light of day under the impulse of a Neapolitan aristocrat called Federico Grisone. Grisone's master was Colas Pagano, son of the king of Naples' head rider. He carefully studied the recently rediscovered writings of Xenophon[1] and took up some of the ideas in his own treatise, *Gli Ordini di Cavalcare*[2], although he often betrayed its "gentle and peaceful" spirit. For although he admitted that horses have an intelligence almost capable of reasoning and a well-considered will, he blamed their resistance on bad grace. The training was carried out gently, with patience and following a methodical and wise progression, unless the horse resisted! Grisone did not for a second think that the horse could not understand what was being asked of it: it was, he thought, because the horse is "cowardly, obstinate, angry, malicious…". Anything, it seems, could be justified to make the horse see reason, from showering it with blows, to threatening it with a small bale of burning straw, to a cat tied upside down on the end of a pole and dragged under the horse's stomach and between its thighs, or even to a hedgehog, a dog, or a piece of metal "all covered in spikes" tied underneath its tail.

Nevertheless, his academy became incredibly famous. It was an essential rite of passage to all who wished to reach perfection. Riders and nobility from the whole of Europe came to seek the knowledge and practices of indoor and outdoor riding, as well as those of hippiatry.[3] For Grisone was a "pioneer". He trained the horse to be "accurate and light" and trusting in its rider's hand: the horse could then obey him and, to a larger extent, follow his indications. He wanted the rider's body to "correspond to the horse's spine with similar harmony and concordance as though it were music". This was also new because, until then, the rider was quite separate from his horse, on a big saddle, and therefore hardly aware of the undulations of the horse's back. "To correspond" was to begin to unite, to be at one together. The hand on the reins had to be low and the horse very much in a position of ramener. It had to be exercised on a circle in order to become supple and to obtain a rounded outline. He therefore trained the horse to be collected (that is, to transfer weight onto its hindquarters): it was an education.

Previous page facing
Viennese rider in trot,
on an circle.

To prove the quality of his work, Grisone achieved passage and piaffe, typical Haute École movements, as well as airs above the ground;[4] courbette, croupade, ballottade, capriole.

Another Italian, Cesare Fiaschi, founded an academy of equitation at Ferrare in 1534. Fiasche was first and foremost a precursor in matters of farriery; and the teachings within his book *Trattato dell'imbrigliare, maneggiare e ferrare cavalli* (1556) remained authoritative until the nineteenth century. He advocated training the horse to music, with rhythm. He wrote that "without tempo or measure, nothing good can be done". What's more, his book contains detailed notation of rhythms to be used in the manège. According to him, it was important for the good rider to "know the natural way of a horse he wishes to tame and handle". He disapproved of unresponsive and fearful horses being "usually treated fiercely and harshly", and suggested that highly strung horses should be "soothed and guided with all kindness and softness". Finally, he trained Pignatelli (amongst others), the third Italian great master. Giambattista Pignatelli was born around 1525 and died before the end of the sixteenth century. Accor-ding to one of his students he was "sparing in blows and generous in caresses". He trained illustrious pupils, such as the Frenchmen Salomon de la Broue and Antoine de Pluvinel.

It was from this "Neapolitan core curriculum" that the founders of the French, German, English, Scandinavian and, to complete the circle, the Andalusian and Portuguese schools, spread their wings. But it was in France that this equitation underwent its most impressive development, achieving a rare degree of finesse and mastery in the eighteenth century, under the School of Versailles. In the sixteenth century, the horse was still considered to be a tool. He had to obey and no concessions were made. The rider's authority was unquestionable. If necessary, this authority was established through force with the use of imposing bits and spurs. With the seventeenth century French master riders, the horse became an "intelligent being" that one needed to tame. Gradually, riding became the art "of manipulating balances and imbalances, turning the horse into a creature that was submissive but representative of the intelligence, rather than the brutality of the rider".[5] Technique and art shut themselves away behind the four walls of the arena and were refined towards the difficult airs. A divide began to appear between this type of schooling equitation, restricted to demonstrations, and another more utilitarian and natural type.

Salomon de la Broue (c. 1530 to c. 1610) is often considered the "restorer of French equitation", but a more appropriate term would be "innovator". He imported what he learnt in Italy, but was the first to use his own observations to lay the foundations and establish a doctrine which the printing press would then help distribute. His method was also based on Xenophon's writings but went against the ideas commonly held at the time. For him, the horse did not disobey out of "malice", but through fear of a misunderstood punishment.

Above
Everyday, riders and
horses work in the
solitude of the
schools.

Overleaf
Lipizzaner stallion in
piaffer, on the long
reins: training session
in the Hofburg arena
in Vienna.

It therefore had to be educated with softness, and through that softness, to be led to understand what its rider was expecting. De la Broue condemned the barbaric processes used as so many little "secrets due to a lack of knowledge" and pointed out that even more softness should be used if the horse was stubborn, rather than punishing it. In a groundbreaking approach, he studied the psychology of each horse, rewarded and stroked; this did not stop him however, sometimes, administering blows from the whip on the horse's croup. Psychology did not equal weakness! La Broue pointed out that "a good hand – light, soft and firm – knows to resist and yield appropriately and to control the action of the legs with precision and that this perfection also comes from the seat". In doing so he established what was to become the basis of all (good) horse riding: the harmonious use of the aids. His book, *Le Cavalerice François*, published in 1594 was, along with Grisone's treatise, the most important publication of the seventeenth century on the subject. It was in fact rapidly translated into Spanish, English and even Italian. This modest, wise man  who was keen to train the grooms before teaching the horses, died penniless and without even suspecting the influence he would have in the future. It was with Antoine de Pluvinel (1555-1620) however that French equestrian art was truly born and separated itself from the Italian teachings. A student of Pignatelli, Pluvinel is indeed considered the "father of French equitation". An incredibly gifted, intelligent and skilful master rider, he taught three successive kings, Henri III (1551-89), Henri IV (1553-1610), and then Louis XIII (1601-43). For Pluvinel, a horse's resistance to the rider's wish was due to its ignorance and not its bad volition. One therefore needed to appeal to its intelligence and "work its brains". For this, one had to favour gentleness, and not constraint, for the "horse who handles with pleasure goes with better grace" and "if the horse is impatient, mean and angry, one must avoid beating him as long as he goes forwards". Contrary to Grisone, he "destroyed the strengths" of the neck and "built the hindquarters" by flexing them. As he had observed that the horse had difficulty in turning, he invented the manège pillars and the lunge so as to make the horse work in hand around a single pillar, without tack at first, then with a saddle and stirrups, but unridden. Another characteristic of his teaching was work between two pillars, the aim of which was to lower and build up the hindquarters, to engage the hocks and to generally increase the horse's suppleness. It helped collect the horse and teach it a variety of airs such as the piaffer and the airs above the ground. The horse, tied between the pillars with lunges, under the action of the whip, moves forwards between them up to half way along its body. Stopped by the lunges, its head lowered by the cavesson, the horse cannot stretch and its impulsion is directed upwards for the forehand and on the spot for the hindquarters. Pluvinel therefore practised a highly stylised equitation with the rider sitting very deeply in his saddle. The horse is slowed down to the extreme and heavily balanced on its hindquarters, with its hocks under its mass. This equitation, in all its lightness,

Above
In Lisbon, the riders'
attire bears the arms
of King Don Joa V.
The silk stockings
rise above the knee.

Overleaf
Training session of the
Portuguese School
riders in the gardens
of the Queluz Palace.

The work attire of the Spanish riders is light and adapted to utilitarian equitation such as that carried out on farms. The traditional hat, the rondeño, bears a stripe corresponding to the rider's rank.

precision and elegance, was predominantly destined for the court and the arena. The rider was "straight as he is when on his feet". He had "his stomach forward with a slight hollow near the waist, his knees gripped", the leg was completely dropped, with "the calf stretched and the heel turned to the outside" (because of the spurs). The bits used were more simple, very much softer, and adapted to each horse.

The seventeenth century saw innumerable remarkable master riders: Pierre de la Noue (c. 1580 – c. 16 [?]), Menou de Charnizay (1578–1651), Delcampe (1590-1670), Jean de Solleysel (1617–80), Fouquet de Beaurepère (1600-76), Jean de Saunier (163[?]–17[?]) and so on. But it was during the eighteenth century that equestrian art reached its peak. At that time, theories and research abounded. They were excessive, "chaotic"[6] and even quite often contradictory, as much in doctrine as in principles or methods. The spirit, the style and uses changed: from being rational, riding became scientific. In all the courts of Europe, many carousels put on magnificent shows for the kings' pleasure. Louis XIV, who wanted his horses near him, undertook building work in Versailles. In the Petite and Grande Écuries, which were completed in 1680, he gathered all his school, parade, hunting, travelling, military and driving horses as well as all the staff needed for their care and training. It was from there, the Manège de Versailles, that French equitation exerted its influence throughout the world. In operation until 1830, the Manège de Versailles contributed, in an exceptional

## THE SPIRIT, THE STYLE AND USES CHANGED: FROM BEING RATIONAL, RIDING BECAME SCIENTIFIC.

manner, to the glory of skilful horse riding. It established the so-called "classical" French doctrine, and a multitude of great riders were trained or taught there. Ironically, François Robichon de la Guérinière (1688-1751), who best symbolises and most brilliantly contributed to this worldwide influence of French equestrian art, taught very little in Versailles: only a few hours at the very end of his life. He nevertheless devoted his entire life to his art and remains one of the greatest masters in the history of equitation. His book, *École de Cavalerie*, published in Paris in 1729, is considered to be the "equestrian bible".

In 1715, armed with letters of marque as crown equerry, La Guérinière settled in Paris and, in association with Jean-François Colménil,[7] created an academy. Their aspiration was to build an academy that "by the beauty of its arenas, the grandeur of its stables and the number of its rooms, would be the only one of its kind in Paris"[8]. The equestrian academies of the time were nothing like our present riding schools. Their role was to train the nobility. The art of equitation was taught by a respected master, together with fencing, music, dance or elements of mathematics, leading on to the art of fortifications. These academies mostly aimed to develop the moral, intellectual and artistic qualities

Opposite
Cadre Noir rider
performing a pirouette
in canter.

Above
Warming up on long
reins, on the tracks of
the French National
Riding School.

of young noblemen (self-control, observation of others, control of one's emotions and reflexes, the acquisition of patience, calmness, courage, humility, determination etc.) in order to place them at the king's service. The art of horse riding was the keystone of this apprenticeship as it is a true education "whose aim is to elevate (the soul), to instruct (to teach) and to shape (the body and spirit). [...] The horse is no more than a creature of flesh and blood [...] it is equally a symbol (of power and skill) in that it allows man to metamorphose it, that is to say, in the strongest possible terms, to bring on a succession of deaths and resurrections leading to the perfection of matter, here the horse".[9] But whereas the masters passed their knowledge down to a restricted number of pupils, in an individual, intimate, secret, almost esoteric manner, La Guérinière promoted a "natural and carefully thought out", transparent, methodical, rational equitation at the service of the masses. He chastised empirical riders, those who weren't demanding of themselves, who were content with mediocrity, or who practised through imitation. He wrote, "without theory, the practice is always uncertain. Theory teaches us to work by following good principles and these principles, rather than go against nature, must serve to perfect it with the help of art". The scientific approach, which applied in all domains, began to play an important part in equitation, and with La Guérinière, as in all sciences, principles (theory) became the founding elements. Colménil and La Guérinière parted ways in 1724. Having become a royal equerry, La Guérinière was eventually appointed

director of the Manège des Tuileries in 1730 by France's Master of the Horse, Prince Charles of Lorraine, Count of Armagnac, who reopened the school for him even though it had been closed since 1680, the date when the royal stables were moved to Versailles. He worked there until his death and came to know global acclaim. The first volume of *École de Cavalerie* appeared in 1729, the second in 1731 and then, *Éléments de Cavalerie*, a sort of abridged version of *École de Cavalerie*, in around 1740. All his works were immensely successful and were reprinted several times during his lifetime. Although it is more of an encyclopaedia of equestrian knowledge, including veterinary medicine, rather than a scholarly treatise of equitation, *École de Cavalerie* is a particularly remarkable piece of work. "The order of the chapters, the development of the doctrine and of its applications, the definitions and the formulas charm the reader as a result of their clarity and the ease of the sentence. The rider will find within it all that he can acquire on his own, on the condition that he should be prepared to read carefully and that he should no longer be a beginner. Within it, the rider delves back into a revision of the knowledge placed equidistantly between Xenophon's ancient asceticism and Steinbrecht's Germanic scrupulous minutiae".[10] The rider's position was of vital importance. Until then it had changed little. The saddles allowed for very little movement and the rider was wedged between the relatively high battes (front and back parts) of the saddle, in a position which limited his movement: the body was straight, the small of the back was hollowed and the rider sat on the front of

Below
In the stables of the
School of Jerez.

Right page
Rider of the Cadre
Noir de Saumur, after
work, at dawn.

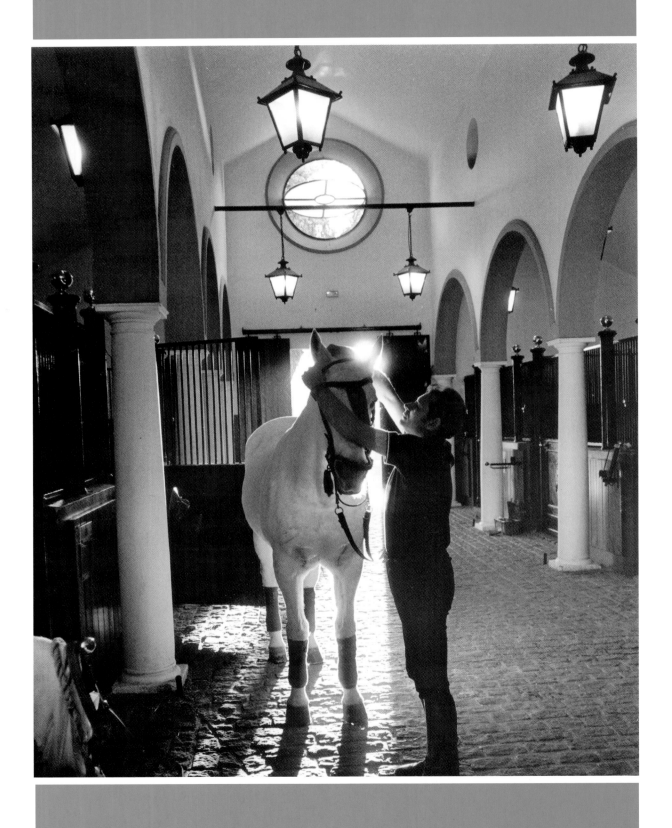

his saddle "upon the buttocks which must not be used on horseback".[11] The thighs and the knees formed a vice, the rider's position required strength and he sought his balance in this arched position, as though, as Pluvinel described it, "he is afraid to be sat"! Flexibility existed only in the upper body, "free with all possible sincerity, and the leg is placed neither too close and neither too far, holding the horse's belly under the threat of a formidable spur". La Guérinière modified the saddles and asked the riders to adjust their horse's balance using… their seat. This required beauty, precision and effectiveness: "grace is a great adornment for the rider […] by grace I mean an air of ease and freedom that must be kept within a straight and free posture, whether it be to hold and strengthen oneself on the horse – at all gaits – when necessary, or to appropriately relax, whilst maintaining, as much as possible, within the horse's movements, that accurate equilibrium that depends upon the counter-balance of the well kept body and for the rider's movements to serve more to embellish his seat than to seem to be helping his mount."[12]

La Guérinière sought "perfection" – for the horse to recapture, under the saddle, the lightness and grace that it possesses naturally. Increasing the suppleness of the horse formed an essential part of this, which in turn required the consideration of their nature, different depending upon the individual, and the understanding of the reasons for their resistances. The rider should "never act in temper or anger", appropriate "punishment", given at the right time, being sufficient. He finished, as though trying to ram this notion into the student's head, by stating

## LA GUÉRINIÈRE SOUGHT "PERFECTION"; FOR THE HORSE TO RECAPTURE, UNDER THE SADDLE, THE LIGHTNESS AND GRACE THAT IT POSSESSES NATURALLY.

"the gentle use of aids and of punishments is one of the most beautiful qualities of the horseman".

For training, he condemned the use of force. Working in trot is "the foundation of the basic suppleness and basic obedience that one must give to horses" and suppleness, obedience and lightness are key points. To work in trot and on the circle, to halt, rein back and to perform various transitions, to truly increase the suppleness of the horse, to render it agile and obedient, two lessons are needed, both of which are considered to have been invented by La Guérinière (or, at the very least, he codified them): the shoulder-in and the release of contact. Although it is likely to have been his instructor, M. de Vendeuil, who "invented" the shoulder-in, it was La Guérinière who defined and promoted it. This lesson, "which is the most difficult and the most useful of all those that one must use to flex a horse", follows on from de la Broue and Newcastle's work on the circle and lateral work. It is used in the three gaits and "produces so many good effects at once that I see it as the first and last of all those that can be given to the horse to help it acquire total wwwsuppleness and perfect freedom in all its parts. This is so true that a horse that will have been flexed following this principle and spoiled after or at the School, or by some

Below and opposite
Although the
foundations are
identical, each type
of equitation is
characterised by
the type and aptitudes
of the horse used.
Sport horses carry
themselves forwards
while the Andalusian
is predestined for
collection.

ignoramus, when put back to this lesson for a few days by a horseman, will be found to be as supple and able as before."[13]

The release of contact is the ceasing of all hand and leg action which places the horse in "supervised freedom". It is invaluable "in as much as it calms the horse, allowing it to maintain a moist mouth and to relax its jaw. […] It is often effective to the point of restoring complete harmony: the horse yields immediately and chews its bit […]. It can only be done on a very well trained horse that has such perfect balance and such control of its paces that it will remain, for the longest time possible, in the same attitude, the same tempo, displaying the same level of energy without being prompted by the rider's aids."[14]

The shoulder-in and the release of contact are, without a doubt, the most important innovations of the French School. They took La Guérinière and the School of Versailles to very high echelons of dressage, with levels of refinement, gentleness and panache that extended French equestrian art into all the courts of Europe.

Of course, de la Broue, Pluvinel or La Guérinière were not the only great master riders of their time. But they illustrate and symbolise the height of research, intellectual innovation and of the equestrian practice of their century, as much in technique as in the relation of man to horse. Many other horsemen of equal talent, some remembered by history, others forgotten, also played a part in this impetus and the birth of this art.

Nevertheless, thanks to La Guérinière, the eighteenth century reached the peak of poetry of movement and of a controlled art. From La Guérinière and his book, from this common seed, the great schools of Vienna, Saumur, Lisbon and Jerez were born and subsequently developed, each with their particular uniqueness and with own individual future.

The curb bits worn
by the Lipizzaners of
the Spanish Riding
School in Vienna are
decorated with the
imperial arms.

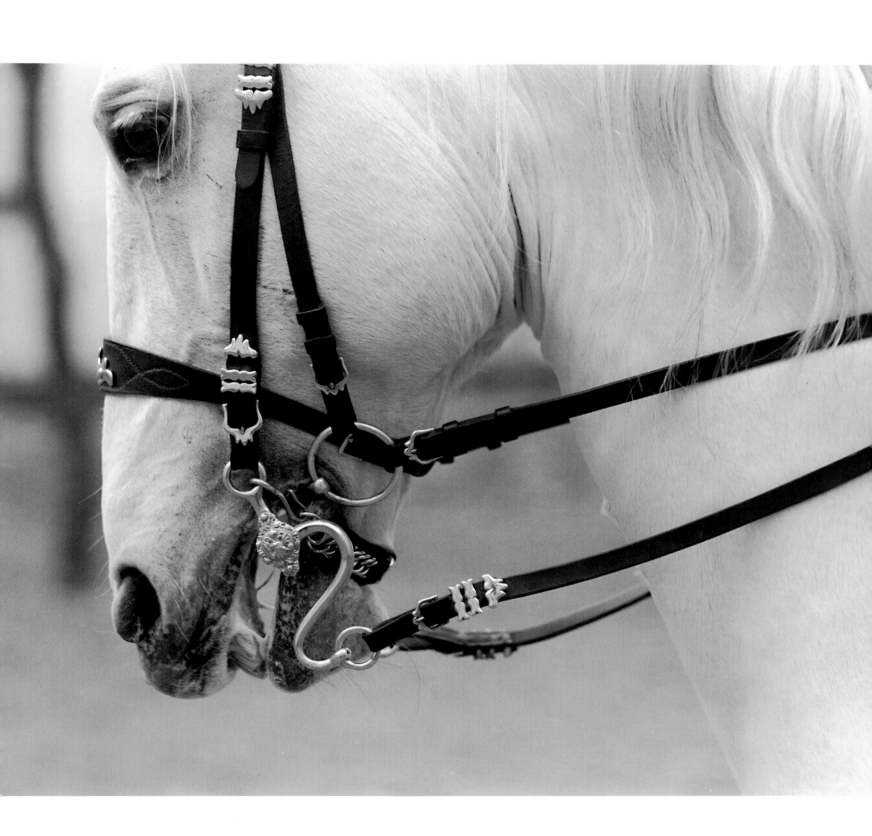

# SRV

The Spanish
Riding School
in Vienna

The Spanish Riding School in Vienna is the oldest of the four. Although the School officially dates back to the eighteenth century, the first document citing a "maneige espagnol" is from 1572 and one can reasonably think that an arena (probably made from wood) was already in existence well before then.

The Archduke Charles, brother of Emperor Maximilian II (emperor from 1564 to 1576), asked his cousin Philippe II, king of Spain, for a number of Andalusian stallions and broodmares, as these horses were reputed to be "the most intelligent, the boldest, the most generous... and the most docile in the manège".[1] He first set his stables up in Kladrub in Bohemia (1562), then in Lipizza (now in Slovenia) where, in 1580, he founded the stud which provided the School with horses until 1918[2] and gave its name – Lipizzaner – to the horses it produced.

Maximilian II founded a school in Vienna in 1572 called the Spanish School. This was because only horses of Spanish origin were accepted. At this point, the history of the School began. Closely tied to the cultural, economic and political life of Austria, from the Habsburg Empire to the Republic, it followed and endured its glories as well as its misfortunes.

The arena had three walls, the fourth side being made up of a row of columns. The master riders worked there every day to train the horses for Haute École. In 1658, when Leopold I acceded to the throne, baroque art experienced unprecedented brilliance and splendour. The equestrian ballets were a great success. Being a great music lover, and to celebrate his wedding with the Infanta Marguerite-Thérèse, daughter of Philippe IV, king of Spain, he had a wooden opera built, which could contain five thousand people. Around 1300 people and hundreds of horses trained in Haute École danced there with a radiance and richness that, according to contemporaries, was beyond anything that had been seen before. In 1681, as the "old" arena was completely dilapidated, Leopold I took the decision to have another built in the same place.

The foundations were dug that very year, the roof in 1683, the horses were working but the school could not be finished: Vienna was besieged by the Turks, whose artillery bombarded all buildings (including this manège).

After the war, there was no money left. It wasn't until 1722 and the reign of Charles VI that the work was completed. However, as the purpose of the building had changed (it was taken up by the Court's library and vehicles), the Spanish School still did not have a fixed location. Charles VI therefore decided to build the Winter arena (where the School still performs today), known as the Winter Riding School (Winterreitschule), where the imperial family's ornamental garden used to be (it was devastated by the Turks in 1529 then turned into a track for tournaments). Fifty-five metres long, eighteen metres wide, seventeen metres high and completely white, it was inaugurated on the 14th of September 1735 and reached four stories high: "its outside façade is improved by a row of double columns and the edifice is topped by a dome extending into a sloping roof.

Above and
previous page
The magnificent
Hofburg arena
in Vienna.

A stone slab, on the round arch, bears the Latin inscription of the name of the builder and the School's mission statement: built [...] with the aim of teaching and training the noble youth, and [...] to develop horses for academic and military equitation".[3] The first balcony is linked to the second by forty-six Corinthian columns. Opposite the riders' entrance, the royal box dominates the whole structure. Since 1743, it has been decorated with a portrait of Emperor Charles VI, riding a Lipizzaner, which the master riders salute every morning as a sign of appreciation.

This arena was the setting for many spectacular parties. Between each of these, the daily work of the Lipizzaners continued. Few foreigners received its training and only on condition of being of aristocratic origin or of descending from military families. The last carousel took place on the 21st of April 1894. For the first time, non-noble officers participated, as well as employees of the imperial and royal School of equitation.

During the First World War, the horses were evacuated from Lipizza, situated in a combat zone, to Kladrub, in Bohemia, and Luxenburg, near Vienna. After the war, Italy received some of the horses and brought them back to Lipizza (where they were still being bred), whilst the Republic of Austria finally took over the Austrian Lipizzaners and, in 1920, transferred them to a State stud in Piber, near Graz.

After the First World War and the collapse of the Austro-Hungarian monarchy in 1918, Austria was reduced to a restricted territory and the School, an imperial vestige, faced a very uncertain future. Its dissolution, mentioned many times already, appeared imminent. It only survived (as well as the Lipizza stud) thanks to the courage and tenacity of a handful of men, very attached to the School, such as Baron Eugène Beck von Mannagetta (charged with liquidating the Court's estate) or head rider, Mauritius Hérold, last director of the School under the Empire. The latter employed many personal initiatives, going so far as to create and sell postcards showing the different school airs to... buy stable brooms. Dependent until then on the Grand Equerry, the School and its head rider were now under the responsibility of the Ministry of Agriculture. Thanks to Mannagetta's support, Count Rudolf van des Strasten (appointed director in 1920) took riders on again. To gain revenue, he allowed the public to attend the schooling sessions for the first time and the School performed abroad (Berlin, Aachen, London, The Hague, Brussels).

In 1938 the Nazi army entered Austria and the country became a province of the "Third Reich". Once again, the future of the School was threatened. Thanks to the backing of Austrian generals, it was declared as being under military protection and thus escaped Nazi control. In 1939, a new governor took over its management. A bronze medal winner at the 1936 Berlin Olympic games, he became a symbol: Aloïs Podhajsky. The School's fame having spread and its care for its horses being evident, it benefitted from favourable modifications. The buildings were developed, qualified riders were employed and acquired military status. But political pressures, and then the bombardments, intensified. In 1939, some of the horses were evacuated to the imperial zoo in Lainz. In 1942, all the Piber stud's horses were taken to the Hosteau stud, in Böhmerwald. In April 1945, the whole of the Hosteau stud and its horses were secretly placed into the hands of the American army,[4] then under the control of General Patton (himself a dressage rider having competed in the 1912 Stockholm Olympics) and the last horses remaining in Vienna were sent to Saint-Martin, near Schärding, where the School established itself. All these manoeuvres saved the School and the Lipizzaner breed.

From 1946 onwards, the School was set up in old Dragoon barracks in the town of Wels, in upper Austria, and remained there until its return to Vienna in 1955. Work picked up again. Women could now receive its training and the School resumed its performances abroad as early as 1948: Switzerland, the Federal Republic of Germany, Sweden, England, Denmark, Holland, Belgium, Italy, Spain, Portugal, each time with tremendous success, such as in 1950 at Madison Square Gardens in New York. Following the promulgation of the Constitution of the new Austrian State, the School returned to Vienna and celebrated its reopening on the 26th of October 1955 in the presence of the federal government and the members of the diplomatic corps.

The galas and tours continued. In 1972, the School commemorated the 400th anniversary of its founding and, for the occasion, invited the Cadre Noir of Saumur, directed at the time by Colonel Saint-André. In 1983, an infectious disease killed some thirty horses at the Piber stud. This shock served to further increase awareness of the fragility of the breed. In order to preserve the Lipizzaner, to reorganise and develop its breeding in Austria, the management of the School and of the stud was handed to a single person. The first director was Dr Jaromir Oulehla, famous rider and veterinarian, to whom we most certainly owe the saving of the breed thanks to his achievement in this difficult mission.

During the night of the 26th to the 27th of November 1992, a gigantic fire devastated the buildings situated above and beside the School. Luckily, the horses escaped unscathed, caught and calmed by passers-by in the street.

On the 1st of January 2001, the School (Spanish Riding School, or SRS) and the Piber stud (Bundesgestüt Piber, or BGP), until then under State authority, were privatised and "merged" to form a "company constituted under civil law" (Gesellschaft öffentlichen Rechts), structured like a private limited company.[5] Although belonging to the Austrian Republic and under the guardianship of the Ministry of Agriculture, the SRS-BGP became economically independent. It receives no grants or subsidies. Its funds and resources come from profits made from its shows, its international tours, its guided visits and from the sale of equestrian equipment marketed under the brand name SRS Kollektion.

Despite the lack of money, the wars, the multiple evacuations of the horses,[6] the geopolitical changes, the economic and administrative complexities, the Viennese master riders have been at work every day for over four hundred years, following a rhythm,

Previous page
The carousel of
the Spanish Riding
School in Vienna is
characterised by the
evenness of the gaits
and the perfect
symmetry of the
tracks.

almost a ritual, that remains immovable. They receive young Lipizzaner stallions that they train up to Haute École and regularly perform with. From the education of young aristocracy and their training for war to academic equitation, that is to say art for art's sake, the aims and functioning of the School have remained unchanged. It is an academy whose objectives, in keeping with its origins, are the breeding of Lipizzaners, the dressage of stallions, the respect for the principles of classical equitation and the instruction of master riders. On this last point, the emphasis is placed on the development of the rider's personality and on education in Haute École work, following a method which remains faithful to the Renaissance traditions, although enriched over the years.

## The riders

Each school operates around a director and a head rider. In each one, the head rider fulfils a technical role, while the director takes on the tasks relating to administration, planning, organisation, management etc. These two "heads" work collaboratively. In Vienna, the head (principal) rider is selected by the director. This post is the highest echelon of the master riders' hierarchy. As head of the horses' dressage, of the riders' training and, more widely, of a tradition which is passed down the generations through word of mouth, he will have "grown up" within the institution and received all his education, first hand, from veteran master riders. The director is appointed by the Ministry of Agriculture.

FROM THE EDUCATION OF YOUNG ARISTOCRACY AND THEIR TRAINING FOR WAR TO ACADEMIC EQUITATION, THAT IS TO SAY ART FOR ART'S SAKE, THE AIMS AND FUNCTIONING OF THE SCHOOL HAVE REMAINED UNCHANGED.

Today, the School operates with seventeen riders, exclusively men. This number is not fixed, having been fewer riders in the seventeenth and nineteenth centuries. It varies according to its needs, although it cannot go above approximately twenty. In keeping with the School's origins, the riders are recruited at the age of 15 to 16 years old with the aim of spending their whole career at the School. Initially, and for a long time, they work in the stables, and ride on the lunge in order to acquire balance in the saddle, independence of the aids and to prove their aptitude for classical dressage. They are then mounted according to their talent. After a period of four to six years, during which they receive lessons in theory, languages, etc, they must be capable of breaking stallions in and of riding experienced horses. They then join the equestrian team to receive training which will lead them to school their first horse up to the demands of Haute École. If they fail, they leave the School. If they succeed, they progressively rise in rank, on the decision of the head rider, depending on their abilities and the quality of their work, to become

pupil (Eleve), aspiring rider (Bereiteranwärter), rider (Bereiter), master rider (Oberbereiter), first head rider (Erster Oberbereiter) and head rider (Oberbereiter, Stv. Leiter der Reitschule)

In the past, and up until the early twentieth century, on certain occasions, riders would wear a gala uniform consisting of a red topcoat with a gold border and epaulettes with white breeches. The cocked hat was worn "fore and aft", i.e. the points to the front and to the back. The rider also had a sword. This uniform was dropped at the beginning of the twentieth century. At present, the master riders' uniform, fixed in the nineteenth century, is made up of a brown, waisted, double-breasted coat with gold buttons up to the collar. It is worn for training and during performances. It is worn over very close fitting white deerskin breeches.

The boots are black leather. They are reinforced at the knees and have been glossy since the early nineteenth century. The cocked hat is black and is no longer worn "fore and aft" but "cross wise" and bears a gold stripe punctuated with a brass button. The width of this stripe depends on the rider's rank: narrow for the aspiring rider, wide for the rider and master rider. The gloves are of white leather and the whip is a simple birch switch, symbol of modesty. It is short for young horses, longer for others. Turned up swan-neck spurs are worn, which enable riders to touch the horse without having to draw their heel up. They are only used on horses that are completely familiar with the use of the leg.

**The horses**

Similarly to the Portuguese and Jerez schools, Vienna's work is based upon a specific breed, the permanence and breeding of which it maintains, both directly and by correlation. Like the School in Lisbon, it is both the guarantor and torchbearer for this breeding. The Spanish Riding School of Vienna uses Lipizzaner horses descended from the Spanish horses that the archduke Charles imported in the sixteenth century for the imperial Court to ride, from "horses that will have triumphed from all selections".

Up until the nineteenth century there were piebald, bay, brindle, dun and roan horses. Today, most of the horses are white, although they are born completely black: they become white during the first year of their lives. The basis of the current breed comes from fourteen families of mares and six stock stallions introduced in the eighteenth and early nineteenth centuries: Pluto (white stallion), Conversano (black), Favory (roan), Neapolitano (chestnut), then Siglavy (white) and Maestoso (white). Although the breeding of the Lipizzaner proceeded unhindered for two centuries, the wars (Napoleonic, the First and Second World Wars) followed by the shock of 1983, when an infectious disease killed thirty horses, had devastating consequences.

Now under the aegis of a single man, the management of the School and of the Piber stud attaches great importance to the perpetuation of the breed. Today, the Piber stud owns two hundred and fifty-three horses, of which forty-nine are foals and seventy are broodmares.

Culmination of collection, this Lipizzaner is performing a pesade, one of the most ancient airs above the ground, in which the horse sits upon its hind legs, front legs quietly tucked in.

Presentation of the three head riders. The School's horses are all descended from fourteen families of mares and six stallions introduced in the eighteenth and nineteenth centuries.

Every morning,
the ritual is repeated.
Each rider schools a
stallion, brought to
him in the arena, for
approximately twenty
minutes. Four to
six horses are thus
presented to each of
them every day.

Every year, six of the best three-and-a-half-year-old males are taken to the School to begin their career. The School only uses stallions and currently owns seventy-eight, aged between 4 and 27, worked according to a precise programme which remains unchanged since the origins of the School.

As in each school, the horse can be ridden in a snaffle bridle or a double bridle. For the former, the bit used is usually a Fulmer.

The Fulmer bit is used for young horses, but also for work in hand, on the long reins, in training and in performances. Although the snaffle bridle has a throatlash, the double bridle does not. The double bridle is used in ridden presentations and only on the experienced horses. It is made up of a snaffle bit and an S-shaped curb bit, adorned with the arms of the House of Austria. The cheekpieces of the curb bit, the browband, the (cavesson) noseband and the curb reins are decorated with different brass, or brass plated, motifs. For certain special occasions, the snaffle bridle's cheekpieces and reins are enhanced with a golden stripe.

The work saddle is an English saddle, in brown leather. The show saddle, or school saddle, evolved over time in keeping with the idea the riders had of a correct seat. Today, it has two battes (raised parts), one at the front, one at the back, and is covered in white deerskin. It is held in place by a hemp girth, a crupper and a breastplate decorated with gold stripes. For in-hand work, the stirrups are fastened either side and to the back of the cantle by two little straps.

The saddle cloth is red, highlighted with gold stripes (two for a master rider, three for a head rider). For presentation on the long reins, the horse wears a red pad lined with gold stripes and decorated with the imperial arms: the two-headed eagle with outstretched wings.

The Cadre Noir
in Saumur

This Saumur
jumper (here in
show dress)
is in piaffer.
He will transfer
his balance onto
his hindquarters
in order to execute
a courbette.

Although the Cadre Noir in Saumur was formed only during the first half of the nineteenth century, reaching its definitive structure in the second half, its roots go back to 1593, when Henri de Navarre, the future Henri IV, left Saumur and entrusted Duplessis-Mornay[1] with the mission of founding a protestant university coupled with an equestrian academy. In 1762, a school was built on the Chardonnet, in Saumur, to receive the officers and non-commissioned officers responsible for training within the cavalry regiments. The Saumur School itself came into existence in 1814. It was under its first head rider, M. Cordier, in 1828, that the Cadre Noir presented its first carousel (made up of school and jump movements), on the occasion of the visit of the Duchess de Berry.

The outfits weren't yet black (they became so during the reign of Louis-Philippe), but the riders already wore the lampion, or cocked hat. As its purpose was purely military, the Cadre Noir adapted itself to the needs of its time and, in particular to the evolution of combat. Therefore, the type of riding taught between 1814 and 1822 at the Cavalry School (still strongly influenced by eighteenth century equitation) no longer being in keeping with the new order of 1829, it gave way, whether they liked it or not, during the nineteenth century, to a campaign-style of riding, known as military, with its own special characteristics. Although the master riders had a passion for Haute École, they excelled in all disciplines and were as capable of breaking a

horse in or of training a jumper as of training a horse for Haute École or of training a horse for battle. In particular, they developed their horses' boldness, their courage and their endurance in the "new disciplines" (racing and cross country) which boomed after the Franco-Prussian war of 1870. Indeed, the advent of quick reloading weapons, smoke-free gunpowder and long range artillery militated aigainst cavalry charges and the nature of combat was profoundly altered: they needed to find increasingly hot-blooded horses, with both speed and endurance. Thus the master riders increasingly devoted themselves to flat, jump and trot racing: "Other than the horse selection, based on speed, that it brings about, racing, that most aristocratic of sports, develops qualities, both on and off track, useful to all horsemen, whether it be pace, the reflex of impulsion or the art of bringing a horse to peak condition for war or sport. It develops the taste for measured risk-taking, teaches self-control and cultivates a spirit of quick decision-making, virtues which are necessary to the war leader."[2]

In 1877, the School acquired the Verrie grounds, where natural (cross country) jumps "grew" and became the most selective of France. Between challenges, meant to prove their courage (such as jumping over a table at which other riders were dining or over a railway track as the train was approaching…), the riders shone in all fields of outdoor riding and took part in numerous endurance trials. For example, in 1902, Captain de Saint-Phalle, a remarkable Haute École master rider, won the first war-horse championships, forerunner of three-wday

Above
Firmly oriented
towards sport, the
Saumur School has
always displayed the
work of its young
horses, in particular
on the long reins.
Opposite
Capriole on the
"carriere des écuyers"
(riders' outdoor
school) in Saumur.

eventing. Up until the First World War and then between the two wars, the Saumur Manège experienced exceptional development: it trained brilliant master riders, many of whom found fame, such as General Wattel.[3] It produced endless carousels, organised courses in advanced equitation to encourage officers to ride competitively and distinguished itself on international competition circuits. In 1924, Major Lesage[4] won the individual dressage bronze medal at the Olympic Games in Paris. In 1932, he was individual gold medallist at the Los Angeles Olympics with his horse Taine, and team gold medallist with Major Marion and Captain Jousseaume.

After the Second World War, the Manège was directed for a few months by Major de Minvielle, then by Captain Margot (who held the position of head rider for the longest, from 1946 to 1959). Despite his predecessors' considerable work, thanks to which a core of trained horses and educated master riders remained, the reorganisation of the Manège was difficult. Indeed, other than finding horses (again) and obtaining equipment (again), the problem of recruiting riders arose as well as that of the usefulness and the role of the Manège in the middle of the twentieth century. It was the equestrian eclecticism, the diversity of talents and the master riders' results in top level competitions that allowed the Cadre Noir to survive and to overcome the biggest obstacle: the modern era. This was because, by sounding the death knell for the cavalry, the Second World War, followed by the dissolution of the last Spahis regiment in 1962, almost ended this corps of instructors specialised in the training of horses and riders. Its experts found a second wind in the boom of horse riding within the civilian world. A boom to which the managers of the Cadre Noir, and of the army in general, responded with audacity, modernity and a truly visionary talent. Whilst maintaining its prestigious and vivid academic tradition, Margot encouraged racing – in which officers rode once more – and, above all, eventing. He organised retraining courses and courses for trainers, instructors and professors. The master riders distinguished themselves once more in international competitions. Colonel Lair succeeded Margot in 1959. He maintained the military spirit, the competitive riding and also eased access to some of the training and courses for civilians. In 1964 he was replaced by Colonel de Saint-André. The master riders increasingly took part in international show jumping, dressage and eventing competitions. In 1968, Saumur-trained Chief Warrant Officer Guyon won the eventing gold medal at the Olympic Games in Mexico on his horse Pitou.

Up until 1969, the Cadre Noir was a department of the École d'application de l'arme blindée et de la cavalerie (School of implementation of armoured weapons and cavalry). That same year it entered one of the most difficult chapters of its history. An agreement was made with the French Equestrian Federation: the Cadre Noir remained in Saumur, it kept an organisation and a functioning subject to military hierarchy, but from then on, it was associated with the Institut National d'Équitation (National Institute of Equitation), recently created

The terre-a-terre is a two-beat gait during which the horse gathers its strength to prepare for the capriole, the most classic Haute École jump.

(1968) by virtue of the increasing popularity of equestrian sports. The Institute was placed under the supervision of the Prime Minister and was managed by Colonel Challan-Belval. Despite opposition from the head rider, the Cadre Noir was "de-militarised". The master riders were placed on special service and the School definitively took on the name of Cadre Noir. Their mission was training, participation and demonstration. In 1972, the École Nationale d'Équitation (ENE) (National School of Equitation) was created. Now a public organisation, under the supervision of the Ministère de la Jeunesse et des Sports (Ministry for Youth and Sports), its mission is to professionally train instructors, to participate in the development of the sport and to maintain French equestrian tradition. It is also involved in pedagogic research, serves as a learning resources centre specialised in the education in and practice of horse riding, and ensures the maintenance and influence of French equestrianism.

As head rider from 1975 to 1984, and then director of the ENE from 1984 to 1989, Major Durand (now a General) proved to be one of the driving forces behind the School's development. By reconciling tradition with the present and the future, he was able to give the Cadre its strategic plan and to give it the impetus required for it to succeed. An incredible rider, the last chosen by Margot, winner of the bronze medal in eventing at the European Championships in Harewood in 1959 and at the Rome Olympics in 1960, selected for the 1972 Olympics in show jumping and having an impressive record of achievements in show jumping, Major Durand wanted a "sporting

IN 1984, THE CADRE NOIR'S HORSES, STILL STABLED IN THE TRADITIONAL PREMISES IN THE CENTRE OF SAUMUR, WERE MOVED TO THE ENE.

Cadre Noir, soul of an eclectic School". For him, French equitation, inherited from the cavalry, is founded upon principles which apply to dressage, considered an end in itself, but also to all disciplines. Under him, it was not unusual to see school horses jumping a few fences at the end of a training session or galloping on the tracks. Keen to open the School up, he travelled widely and invited the greatest masters and champions of the time to come to Saumur. These included the expert Nuno Oliveira, the Americans Kusner and Morris, Willi Schultheiss, Hans Winkler, Campion from Ireland, etc. He even had the traditional choreography and music of the performances changed in order to remain in keeping with modernity.

In 1984, the Cadre Noir's horses, still stabled in the traditional premises in the centre of Saumur, were moved to the ENE, in Terrefort. Although it still had a large component on secondment from the Ministry of Defence, it was now the Minister for Sports, after consultation with his Defence counterpart, that chose the head rider. That same year, and for the first time, two women joined the Cadre: Florence Labram and Mireille François (there are now three women wearing the uniform).

In 1986 the Cadre Noir was officially recognised. Lieutenant-Colonel Durand was replaced as head rider by Lieutenant-Colonel de Beauregard, a magnificent rider, then by Colonel Carde in 1991, Colonel de La Porte du Theil in 1999 and then Colonel Faure in 2007.

The Cadre Noir's uniqueness lies in the fact that it has always adapted to its time. Thus, for over a century, its master riders have been influenced by sport and competition. Perhaps the biggest accolade made to the School over the last few years, one that truly marks its history, is the establishment of the Pôle France and the Pôle Espoir (national high level training centres) in Saumur in 2001.

Hence the School is all the more at the service of sport and of the French teams in all three Olympic disciplines. Today, the ENE has over three hundred horses, fifteen Olympic-sized outdoor schools, over fifty kilometres of dedicated tracks, several hundred jumps, seven indoor schools including six Olympic-sized ones, a modern veterinary clinic, a fully equipped amphitheatre and an impressive multimedia library.

The Cadre Noir is now totally integrated into the ENE, particularly since all the School's professors now wear the uniform (since 1999). Together, the Cadre Noir and the ENE represent an international centre for excellence in education, research and competition. They organise many international competitions (eventing, dressage, etc) while the master riders themselves compete at the highest level (Didier Courrèges and Arnaud Boiteau, for example, were team eventing Olympic champions in 2004).

The Cadre and the ENE are involved in many international exchanges. The School welcomes foreign riders on its Course in advanced equitation, it hosts national teams such as the national eventing team of Qatar that came to train for a year in preparation for the 2006 Doha Asian Games – which it won – and, more recently, a Chinese team for the 2008 Beijing Olympics. Conversely, the School's instructors travel all around the world for technical and pedagogic lectures and also participate in the European equestrian training programme, Euroride. The School now incorporates a modern research centre. It carries out studies and research within various technical, scientific or pedagogic domains in order to improve the teaching and practice of equitation. It is responsible for developing the Persival programme (an equestrian simulator which has been successfully brought to the market) and organises several conferences each year.

From a military corps, the Cadre Noir and the ENE have become a state-of-the-art international equestrian university which nonetheless perpetuates the training, presentation and dressage of horses "à la Française".

### The riders

At Saumur, with the exception of Cordier[5] and d'Aure,[6] the head rider is always a military person on active service. Today, the appointment is made by the Minister for Sports after consultation with the Ministry of Defence and the Ministry of Agriculture. The École Nationale d'Équitation, founded in 1972,[7] was run by officers until 1988.

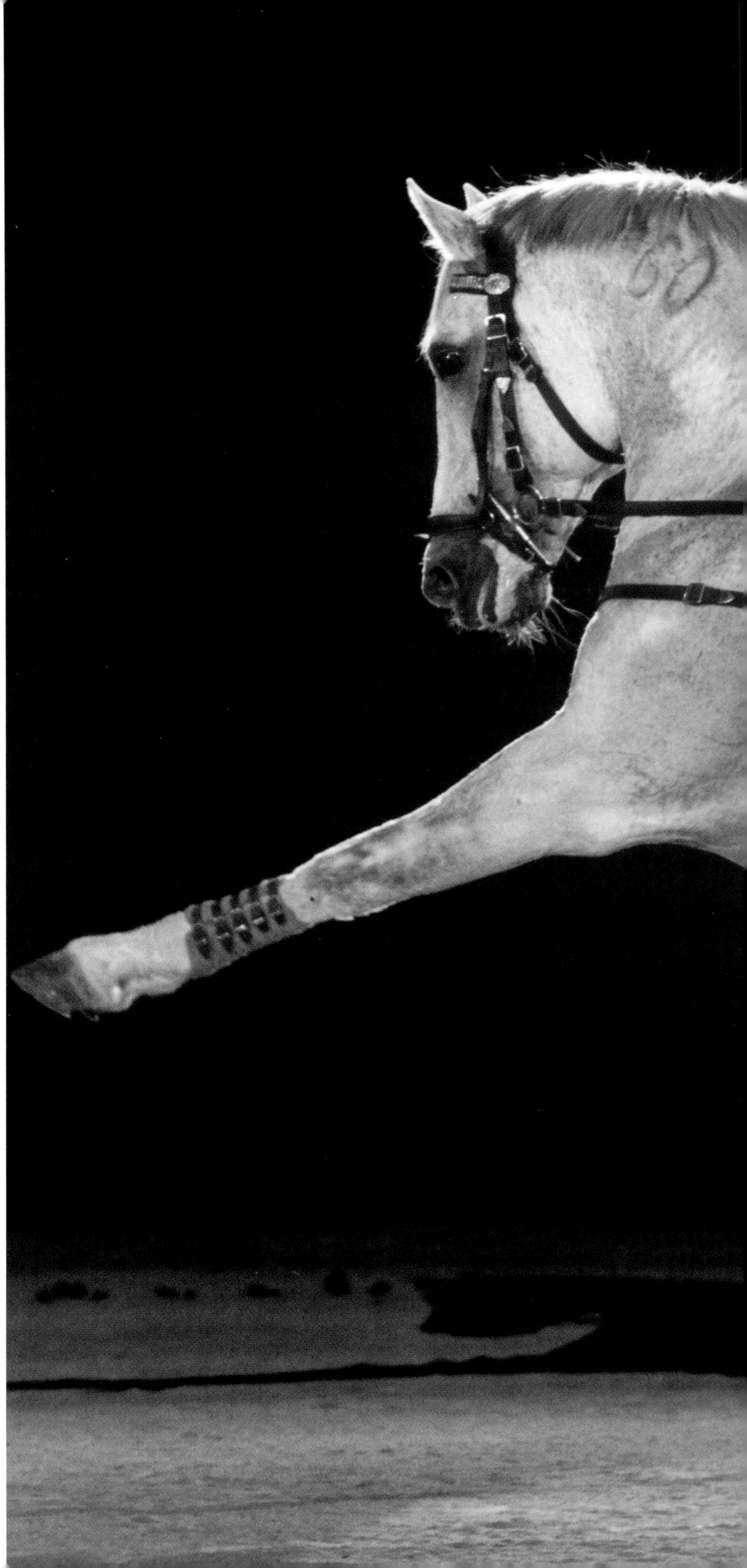

Previous pages
Rider in gala uniform.
The horse wears
gala tack and a
saddle "à la
Française".

Opposite
Saumur's
eclecticism is at
the heart of its
uniqueness.
At the end of
the 1980s, the
ENE acquired a
Lusitano horse,
Odin, here in
Spanish walk
during a Cadre
Noir gala.

Since then, the director of the ENE is a civilian, always a civil servant, chosen by the Ministry for Youth and Sports.

Unlike the other schools that run with about fifteen master riders, Saumur today has forty-three, of whom nine are servicemen. This exception dates from 1999. Before then, it was necessary to distinguish the Cadre Noir master riders – of which the numbers did not exceed twenty – from the other rider-teachers of the ENE. It was the "fusion" in 1999 of the Cadre Noir and the ENE which led to the increase in this number, which resulted in restoring the original quantity, as the Cadre Noir's ranks had previously comprised approximately forty officers and non-commissioned officers until 1939.

Saumur has one special feature: women. In 1984, two women joined for the first time: Florence Labram[8] and Mireille Belot-François.[9] Today, there are three: Nadège Bourdon,[10] Laurence Sautet[11] and Pauline Basquin.[12] Although the Jerez School also includes one woman member, Mrs Bethléem Bautista,[13] those of Lisbon and Vienna are exclusively masculine.

Contrary to the other three schools, Saumur recruits riders who have high level professional credentials. In fact, the servicemen are transferred for four to ten years, while the civilians are recruited by competitive examination. All are appointed by the director upon the head rider's recommendation. Generally, they are at instructor level (BEES2), have trained one or more horses up to Prix Saint-Georges, or have attained good results in national level competitions. During the training period, the student rider will

UNLIKE TO THE OTHER THREE SCHOOLS, SAUMUR RECRUITS RIDERS WHO HAVE HIGH LEVEL PROFESSIONAL CREDENTIALS.

become deputy-rider, rider and, possibly, master rider. The progression occurs over the evolution of competition results, diplomas obtained during continuing education and the validation of knowledge acquired through experience. He could then be appointed head rider by the Minister for Sports after consultation with the Ministry of Defence.

The master riders' outfit has evolved over time. When the Manège was created, Mr Cordier chose a long-tailed black coat, highlighted with gold lanyards and embroidery, as well as a lampion which remained the Cadre Noir's exclusive hat. Previously worn by anyone who rode in a school, this cocked hat had the particular feature of helping the instructor know, at a glance, which riders were looking straight ahead and were holding their head "free and clear from the shoulders". The Second Empire saw the master riders' tailcoat change into a tunic. The Third Republic gave them a kepi (peaked cap), when in service dress, then a frogged Hungarian jacket in 1884 and then eliminated the gold lanyards. The tunic returned in 1901.

Although the official colour of the uniform was dark blue, General L'Hotte[14] and his master riders were already wearing black whereas the military instructors wore a kepi with a light blue cap-band.

Previous pages
In Saumur, work
on the long-reins
forms an integral
part of the show
jumping horse's
training.

Above and opposite
Traditionally, Saumur's
jumpers are Selle
Français or
Anglo-Arabs.

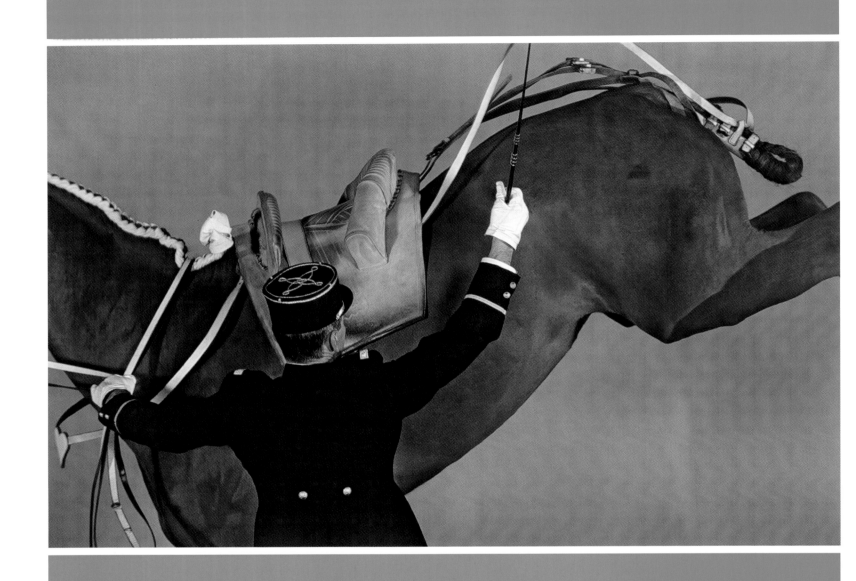

Jumpers' hind
hooves are not
shod and their
tail isplaited and
tied up so as
not to whip the
handler's face.

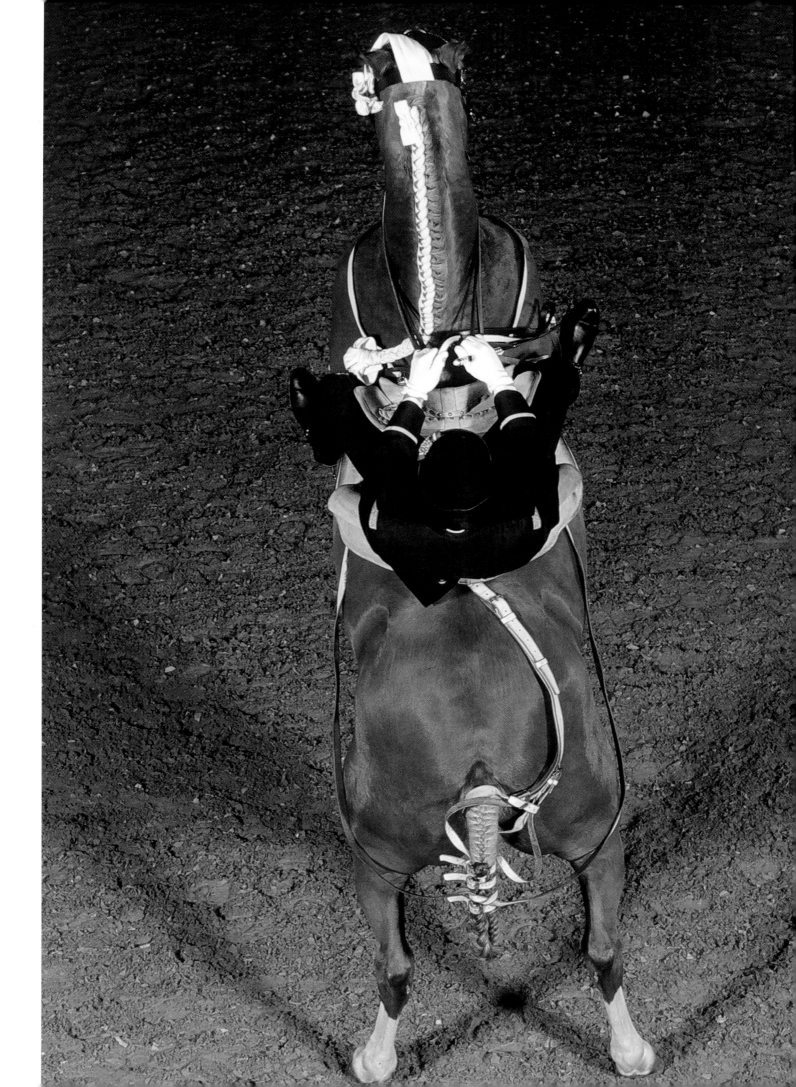

The school horse
is attentive and
concentrated on
the rider's aids. The
tempo and action
of the gait must
be impeccable.

Already, the "Cadre Noir" denoted the riding instructors, while the "Cadre Bleu" denoted the military instructors.

Since 1999, all the ENE's equitation instructors now wear the black uniform. There are four uniforms, each worn depending on the different events:

– the grand gala uniform is worn in the presence of heads of state and monarchs, as was the case in April 2004, in front of Queen Elizabeth II of England. The grand gala uniform is made up of: a black tunic, white breeches, a school hat and pendant medals (the horse wears gala tack);

– the gala uniform for official presentations: black tunic, black breeches, school hat with medal ribbons (the horse wears gala tack);

– the demi-gala uniform for the School presentations on weekdays: it is the same as the previous uniform but the horse's mane is loose;

– the work uniform: black tunic, black breeches and kepi or competition helmet (the horse's mane is loose).

The black tunic is closed with nine buttons at the front and two at the back. These buttons bear a grenade for the servicemen and a sun, symbol of the influence of the Cadre Noir, for the civilians. It remains "one of the most elegant and practical: dark, to allow silhouettes to stand out better, black, for a slimming effect and to enforce correctness…, it draws its value from its severity and simplicity".[15] Its stand-up collar encourages good, upright posture.

The sun also adorns the bits worn by horses in presentation, the civilians' collar facings, their kepis and their buttons. The servicemen have a grenade on their collar facings, on their buttons and on their kepi. The symbols that the servicemen and civilians do have in common are their shoulder flashes and the cross on top of their kepi. The stripes are worn on the sleeves and at the top of the kepi or on the left of the cocked hat. A student rider wears one stripe, a deputy-rider wears one stripe and a second, narrower stripe. A rider wears a stripe and two narrow stripes whilst a master rider has a stripe and three narrow stripes. The cocked hat is adorned with a golden band that passes over a red, white and blue cockade.

Finally, the gloves, of a "Saumur" cut, are cream-coloured. The whip is the regulation cavalry whip, in black for the Cadre Noir, and decorated with golden ferrules. The spurs are copper coloured (worn by golden spurs are Generals).

**The horses**

Unlike the other schools, whose work is based on a very precise breed of horse (Iberian or of Iberian origin), the Cadre Noir does not serve to preserve or promote a particular breed, but instead to promote the results of French breeding as a whole. A report by Colonel de la Porte du Theil[16] indicates that the École Nationale d'Equitation owns three-hundred and fifty horses in its stables, of which seventy-five percent are Selle Français. The remaining twenty-five percent are made up of Anglo-Arabs, English Thoroughbreds, AQPS, one Alter-Real, a Lusitano and several foreign dressage horses (German, Dutch etc). The Cadre Noir's mounts are therefore very varied.

Above
Cadre Noir riders
perpetuate the
school jumps and the
classical riding which
appeared during the
Renaissance; but
above all they are
instructors, teaching
a modern and
sporting equitation.

Today, Selle Français horses are increasing within the ENE's stables due to a number of factors such as the structuring and development of French breeding during the nineteenth and twentieth centuries, the relatively low purchase price of these horses (compared to other breeds) and the School's educational purpose which requires reliable and steady horses for instruction (a task which the Selle Français fulfils). That being so, hot blooded horses, such as those sought by the directors since 1870, constitute the main part of the current competitors' core team. Generally, forty horses are retired each year. The School purchases the same amount annually from French breeders – geldings and mares, aged between three and four years old and already broken-in. It can occasionally buy older horses – depending on their sporting career – but this remains very exceptional. Each horse has its own double bridle and saddle. The cheekpieces of the curb bit, as well as the bits themselves, are the same for the school horses as for the jumpers. The double bridle is made of black leather and its browband is decorated with a small golden chain. Its buckles are golden and, on either side of its mouthpiece, the curb bit features a Gorgon's head, whose stares must have petrified the adversary in time of combat! The bradoon's cheekpieces and reins are, however, different for schooling horses and jumpers: they are white leather for the jumpers and amaranthine for the school horses. For the head rider, the bits, bradoon cheekpieces and bradoon reins are golden.

The school saddle copies the saddle à la Française, established under Louis XIII. Made from light-coloured suede, it is known as "flat" as it does not have a batte (raised part) at the back. That of the head rider is in amaranthine velvet. The saddles are equipped with wide tread stirrups with a grille-tread, also dating back to Louis XIII. They are teamed with an amaranthine and gold saddle cloth, and are held in place by black leather breastcollars and cruppers with golden buckles.

The jumper's saddle is a selle-a-piquer, similar to those used in the Middle Ages during tournaments: the battes at the front and back serve to keep the rider in the saddle, in particular at the moment of the "piquer" (impact) during a joust, which gives its name to this saddle.

Although both these saddles are almost identical to their original models, they have both undergone numerous technical improvements which make them much more comfortable for both horse and rider today.

Jumpers' tails are plaited and held up by two white leather straps tied to the girth in order to prevent it from whipping the handler's face during jumps. Finally, the jumpers' breastcollars, girths, cruppers and tailguards are white.

One of the Cadre Noir horses' special features (inherited from the School of Versailles) is the plaiting of their manes. Achieved using three ribbons, the colours of which match the bradoon reins, it ends in a strand which is knotted and folded to form a rosette at the top of the horse's left shoulder. On the head, a ribbon encircles the left ear and is attached to the browband, ending in a sort of four-petal flower.

A ribbon encircles
the left ear, in a sort
of flower.

# RAJS

The Royal
Andalusian
School of
Equestrian
Art in Jerez

The Royal Andalusian School of Equestrian Art in Jerez, the Real Escuela Andaluza del Arte Ecuestre in Spanish, is located at the heart of Jerez de la Frontera, a town in the south of Andalusia, in Cádiz province, on the plain of the Guadalquivir estuary, famous for its vines (and its sherry) and its horse breeding. Fifth town of Andalusia, it is one of Spain's largest towns. In 2002 it hosted the World Equestrian Games in the seven disciplines recognised by the International Equestrian Federation: show jumping, dressage, eventing, driving, volting, endurance and, for the first time, reining.

In 1970, the year of the School's creation, hardly any Haute École riding remained in Spain, and the art of the manège, as well as that of combat, was no more than a relic. The Spanish horse had lost its stamp of nobility and, throughout Europe, was considered to be nothing more than a leisure horse, in the most pejorative sense, only fit for a few circus tricks. And yet, in the seventeenth century, the Spanish horse stirred the vast and proud crowds on the Plaza del Arsenal, right in the heart of Jerez, by performing Haute École demonstrations – Vueltas escaramuzas a la gineta. Faced with the decline of equestrian art and the disgrace of the Spanish horse, Don Alvaro Domecq decided to found a School which he personally funded during the first five years of its existence. As opposed to Vienna, Saumur or Lisbon, the School in Spain was therefore initially a private venture, intended to promote the Andalusian breed and the Spanish equestrian tradition.

"Combining the class of a Great Spanish Man with the simplicity and finesse of an artist",[1] Don Alvaro Domecq was a big breeder of Spanish horses and bulls. First Spanish *rejoneador*, he was the *alcade* (mayor) of Jerez, deputy to the Cortes and a savvy businessman. His stables housed the future king of Spain's horses and important people came from all over the world to meet them. After a world tour of the great riders, Don Alvaro Domecq devised a meticulous strategic plan. He picked about twenty of his best horses out of the sixty or so which made up his stables at the time, selected high level riders from amongst his closest friends and placed a part of his stables, his manège and members of his stud's staff at their disposal. In order to supervise and follow the work of the horses, he took on a technical director, Doctor Guilherme Borba (who, a few years later, was involved in the creation of the Portuguese School in Lisbon), a breeder of Portuguese horses, himself a great rider and one of the finest students of the great Portuguese master, Nuno Oliveira. The adventure of the Andalusian School had begun.

The quality of the School's equestrian work was rapidly recognised: a selection of its master riders was invited to Austria in 1972 (barely two years after its creation) to celebrate the School of Vienna's 400th birthday alongside the Cadre Noir.[2] In May 1973, King Juan Carlos presented the "Golden Horse" to Don Alvaro Domecq Romero (the founder's son). The "Golden Horse" is the greatest equestrian award given each year in Spain to honour a particularly outstanding rider.

On this occasion and for the first time, on the square in Jerez, the School presented its show, Cómo bailan los caballos Andaluces "How Andalusian horses dance". It revived tradition and had a marquee set up on this very square, where, every day, the general public could witness the work of the master riders and approximately fifty horses, under the direction of Guilherme Borba. From then on, once a month, the School presented its show, whose fame extended far and wide, so much so that they were invited to perform at the Wembley Horse Show, a global celebration of the horse, on the 15th of October 1974, in the presence of the British Royal Family. On the 24th of October 1974, they performed the show at the Manège de l'Étrier, in Paris, and embarked upon a Europe-wide tour.

In 1975, the School having officially been recognised as protector of Spanish equestrian art, the government decided to take on the School's running costs, until then entirely covered by the School's founder. For this, the Ministry for Information and Tourism acquired the Recreo de la Cadenas palace, property of the Duke of Abrantes. This palace, designed and built in 1860 by Rovel, an architect and disciple of Garnier (the architect of the Opéra de Paris) includes an arena and stabling and is surrounded by splendid gardens laid out by its first owner, Julian Penmartin Laborde and inaugurated in 1864 by Queen Isabelle II's husband. Private property until 1975, it became the headquarters for the Andalusian School of Equestrian Art.

To meet the demands of the developing School, a new arena and new stables were built in 1980,

in the palace's park, designed by architect José Luis Picardo. With a main entrance, three lateral doors, space for one thousand and six hundred spectators, a box for twenty-four VIPs and another built for King Juan Carlos and Queen Sofía, the manège is in pure Andalusian style. The stable blocks are arranged around the tack room.[3] Each block is made up of twelve boxes, with a total capacity for sixty horses. Each block bears the name of one of the School's five historic horses that took part in the "Golden Horse" award ceremony: Ruisenor, Vendeval, Garboso, Valeroso, Jerezano.

In 1983, a foundation was set up to manage the School's budget and to put the finishing touches to the School. In 1986, the School created its driving department. In 1987, Don Alvaro Domecq offered his academy to HRH the King of Spain, Don Juan Carlos I. The king accepted, became its honorary president and immediately granted it the name of Royal School of Equestrian Art. Don Alvaro Domecq the younger managed the School. From then on it was entirely publicly funded as the School was placed in the care of five authorities, the most important of which was the regional government of Andalusia which subsidised up to eighty percent of its costs.

In 1990, the Andalusian Government's Council for Tourism and Sport adopted new statutes. From then on, the Regional Council's president became president of the Royal Foundation, which still funds the School today. The Foundation (Fundación Real Escuela Andaluza del Arte Ecuestre) now owns an excellent veterinary clinic (one of the most modern and best equipped in all of Spain),

Above
The Jerez School
horses are plaited
and their manes
are adorned with
four mosquero
(the fourth is on
the forelock).

Opposite
Farm work requires
a submissive,
intelligent and
generous horse.
At Jerez de la
Frontera, the
riders cultivate
this tradition of
utilitarian horse
riding, in particular
in Doma Vaquera.

Above and opposite
For Doma Vaquera,
the rider's outfit is
light, practical and
free: shirt, jacket,
bolero and leather
chaps.

Opposite
Training in the
Arena of the
School in Jerez.

a saddlery workshop and has opened a carriage museum (2002) as well as a museum of equestrian arts (2005). It defines itself as a "social and cultural vehicle for Andalusia's Equestrian heritage". As such it takes on and develops a multitude of activities based around Andalusian horses and culture. Other than the shows (in Haute École and Doma Vaquera) and the highlighting of Andalusia's equestrian heritage, it ensures the promotion and protection of the Andalusian horse and takes part in national and international competitions in driving and dressage (the Royal School counts many high level athletes amongst its master riders, such as Rafaël Soto, dressage team silver medallist at the Athens Olympic Games in 2004 and dressage champion of Spain in 2004). Training has become its mainstay, focussing on Haute École riders, drivers, grooms, saddlers and veterinary assistants (approximately forty students in total across these areas).

**The riders**

Apart from the first, Don Alvaro Domecq, the head rider is appointed upon recommendation by the director of the Royal School's executive committee. He ensures the technical management of horses and riders. The director, who is not a rider, is appointed by the Foundation's management team, made up of:
– the president of the Andalusian government, as president of the Foundation's management team
– the head of the Andalusian Government's Council for Tourism and Sport, as first vice-president
– the president of the Autonomous Community of Cádiz, as second vice-president

## THE SCHOOL BEGAN WITH SIX FOUNDING RIDERS BUT CURRENTLY HAS APPROXIMATELY FIFTEEN, INCLUDING ONE WOMAN.

– the mayor of Jerez de la Frontera
– the head of the Andalusian Government's Vice-Council for Tourism and Sport
– five representatives of the Andalusian Government Council, having a rank of at least general director, and who are each respectively given official duties in terms of professional training, tourism, breeding, culture and continuing training of staff
– two deputies of the Autonomous Community of Cádiz
– the head of the deputation of the Autonomous Community of Cádiz to the Andalusian Government's Council for Tourism and Sport
– a representative of the Ministry of Defence
– a prestigious representative having known achievements in the art of horsemanship, appointed by the management team upon the recommendation of the president. The School began with six founding master riders but currently has approximately fifteen, including one woman, Sra Bethléem Bautista (since 1984). The first master riders were chosen by Don Alvaro Domecq, and, in fact, some are still members of the school today. Since the 1980s, they have been recruited from amongst the riders who complete four years of academic training under the supervision of an experienced master rider in charge of two students. These students are usually young and are admitted

to the School by competitive examination (today, approximately four out of every hundred applicants are accepted). After their training, they only join the School depending on its needs, which tend to be rare. If this is the case they are promoted to basic rider (Jinete), professor rider (Jinete professor) then specialised professor rider (Jinete professor especialiste).

The School has two uniforms, designed by Alvaro Domecq y Romero, its founder, just before its inauguration in 1987 by HRH Don Juan Carlos I, King of Spain: the navy blue gala uniform and the grey striped daily uniform. Eighteenth century Andalusian matador costumes, and in particular those from the town of Ronda, near Granada, inspired the gala uniform. Thus master riders wear leather gaiters and a waistcoat in a macramé of golden sequins, directly inherited from the bullfighting dress code. The gaiters are made of leather, stamped with the royal crown and made by Manuel Roman, the School saddler. They cover brown ankle-boots. The waistcoat is worn over a white shirt with a jabot, complemented by a salmon pink cravat, under a blue bolero with gold detailing. The breeches are navy blue and stop just below the knee where they are held by thin cords with black pompoms that reveal the white stockings. Master riders also wear beige leather gloves and a conical black hat which originally featured a spotted headscarf falling over the nape of the neck. On the hat (the rondeño), the golden band indicates the rider's rank.

The daily uniform follows the same principle except that the short white and black striped jacket is worn over a waistcoat of the same fabric. The cravat is black with white dots and the breeches are black riding breeches.

For Doma Vaquera, each rider is free to choose their outfit within the traditional Andalusian dress code: a white shirt, a waistcoat, a bolero with only the top button fastened and long leather chaps (designed to protect the rider from the bulls' horns). The ladies, sat behind the saddle, wear brightly coloured dresses, such as those worn at the Jerez Féria.

**The horses**

The schools of Vienna, Jerez and Lisbon have in common, amongst other things, that they ride Andalusian horses (or horses of Andalusian ancestry). These horses' morphology perpetuates the movements and balance of those that paraded back in the time of Ferdinand of Aragon's court. Although the explanation for this is historical and particular to each of the Schools, it is impossible to disregard the exceptional accuracy, brilliance and aptitudes of the Iberian horse for classical dressage.

All riders sang, and still sing, its praises: de la Broue, for example, described them as "elite horses". The Duke of Newcastle praised their intelligence,

I T IS IMPOSSIBLE TO DISREGARD THE EXCEPTIONAL ACCURACY, BRILLIANCE AND APTITUDES OF THE IBERIAN HORSE FOR CLASSICAL DRESSAGE.

Overleaf
Jerez School rider
in piaffer.

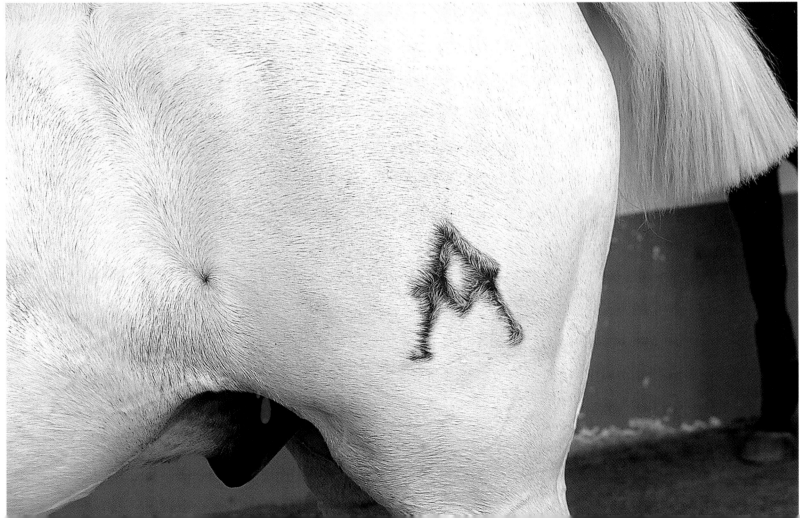

Opposite
In the "Viennese"
courbette,
performed here
by a Jerez
rider, the horse
moves forward
in little jumps,
balanced on
its hind legs.

In general, the
purebred Andalusian
horses come from
the School stud's
stock of broodmares
whilst their sires are
School stallions.
For the most part they
are grey, but some
can be bay or black.

Opposite
The Doma
Vaquera horses
are Anglo-Arabs or
Hispano-Arabs.

Above
The Andalusian
horse has a natural
predisposition for
the collected airs,
such as the piaffer,
shown here.

obedience and courage and wrote of them: "it is the most noble horse in the world, the most beautiful and the most worthy to carry a king on a day of victory". La Guérinière pointed out that all "authors have given preference to the Spanish horse and have seen it as the first for the school (agility, suppleness, cadence), for pomp and parade (pride, nobility, grace), for war (courage and obedience)" adding that some use it for hunting and driving which is unworthy of such a good horse!

The Jerez School owns approximately twenty gelded Anglo-Arab and Hispano-Arab horses for Doma Vaquera, but mostly use purebred Andalusian horses. It owns one hundred and thirty horses aged from four to twenty-two years old, of which eighty are males. They come from the School's own stud, located roughly twenty kilometres away from Jerez (where twenty-seven mares reside, the sires being the Schoolhorses) and from certain private studs. Additionally, each year, between two and four horses come from the military stud, under contract for a period of six years.

The pure-bred Andalusian horses, measuring between 16 and 16.2 hands, are usually grey, although the School owns some bay, chestnut and black horses. All are subjected to rigorous selection and detailed examinations which direct them towards performing, driving, competing, classical dressage, Doma Vaquera, etc. depending on their aptitudes: horses for the airs above the ground require a powerful build, school horses need beautiful paces and Doma Vaquera horses must be naturally calm, attentive and extremely easy to handle in order to later be able to execute the

SCHOOL JUMP WORK REQUIRES HORSES WITH A POWERFUL BUILD, SCHOOL HORSES NEED BEAUTIFUL PACES AND DOMA VAQUERA HORSES MUST BE NATURALLY CALM, ATTENTIVE, AND EXTREMELY EASY TO HANDLE.

movements specific to this discipline. The jumpers and school horses join the School at the age of three and are broken in and trained following a precise programme aiming to develop their musculature and to then train them in Haute École and in the airs above the ground. Similarly to Vienna and Lisbon, they are all stallions, and only the best will get to perform under the spotlights. They are retired around the age of twenty-two, in a property close to Jerez. The double bridle used for the school horses is the same as the one worn by the jumpers. The curb bit cheekpieces, the browband and the noseband are black leather decorated with identical motifs to those found on the saddle cloth. The curb bit is made of steel adorned with the arms of the Spanish monarchy in gold.

During galas, the cheekpieces and reins can be in golden leather. As in Vienna, the double bridle does not feature a throatlash.

The capriole is
an air which all
four Schools
have in common.
It is the pinnacle of
the airs above the
ground and requires
considerable energy
on the part of the
horse.

In the Jerez
manège, the
horse leaps
into the air
and then bucks.
The movement
is all the more
impressive for
being far above
the ground.

Above
Backstage at a
show, a Doma
Vaquera horse
passes a pure-bred
Andalusian horse
in Spanish Walk.

The horse rears
and proceeds in
small successive
leaps. This is the
"Viennese" courbette,
also performed in
Jerez.

The saddle is the same for flatwork and for school jumps. Taking its inspiration from the traditional Spanish saddle, it has a fairly short batte (raised part) at the front and a slightly longer but narrow and low batte at the back. The stirrups are made of iron and are identical to those of the eighteenth century.

The saddle cloth is embroidered with the arms of the Spanish monarchy and features motifs which reappear on the breastplate and on the leather parts of the double bridle. The saddle cloth is navy blue and gold for galas, blue and white, or red and gold for the public shows given at the School. At the front of the saddle, a rolled up rug (manta estribera) in the same colour as the saddle cloth, covers the pommel and falls on either side of the horse's shoulders.

The horses are plaited and wear four mosqueros, strands of pompoms made from natural horsehair: one is fixed to the browband, the three others are distributed across the mane.

The Doma Vaquera horses have special tack. The bridle has no throatlash and is made up of a plain cavesson noseband, a large mosquero on the browband and two reins (as opposed to four for the manège and jump horses) since the rider rides with one hand (the other hand holds the garrocha, a type of long lance used for working with bulls).

The saddle is a traditional work saddle. Made from locally available materials it includes a straw tree wrapped in leather and covered with sheepskin, a very high, rounded cantle and padding filled with horsehair. The stirrups, inherited from the Arabs, are triangular with a wide tread. The stirrup leathers are also wide and are lined in order to compensate for potential breakages. The girth passes all around the horse and under the sheepskin. A crupper keeps the saddle in place. Once more, on the pommel, a black and white manta estribera can be found.

Opposite
Magnificent
"Viennese" courbette.

Overleaf
A demonstration from
the Doma Vaquera
riders in Jerez.

The
Portuguese
School of
Equestrian Art
in Lisbon

The Portuguese School of Equestrian Art is the youngest of the four schools, as it was re-formed in 1979. It is located about ten kilometres from Lisbon, in the national Queluz Palace, ancient country home of the Marquis of Castelo Rodrigo, converted into a royal residence after the eighteenth century restoration and until 1908, when it became State property. It revived the Picaria Real[1] of Belém, created by King Joâo V, king of Portugal from 1706 to 1750. This was the equitation presented by the Royal Court Academy from the eighteenth century up until 1807, the year of its closure due to the Napoleonic wars. In Portugal, horse riding has long been the subject of much research and has its own literature. In 1434, 116 years before Grisone, King Duarte was already penning his *Livro Da Ensinança De Bem Cavalgar Toda Sela* (*The art of riding on every saddle* - translated into English as "The Royal Book of Jousting, Horsemanship and Knightly Combat"). In 1678, Galvào de Andrade published *Arte da cavallaria de Gineta* (*The art of Gineta cavalry*) and, in 1679, Antonio Pereyra Rego completed *Instruçam da cavallaria de brida* (The art of cavalry and the use of the bridle). The masterpiece of equestrian literature, *Luz da Liberal et Nobre Arte da Cavallaria* (*Light of the liberal and noble art of cavalry*), by Manoel Carlos de Andrade, was published in 1790. Directly inspired by the works of the Marquis of Marialva, it gives an account of the equitation practised at the Royal Manège of Belém. At that time, equestrian art was experiencing an admirable lightness and brilliance. The horse was completely submissive, pushed to the limit of its capabilities, in a collaboration based on absolute trust. This result was, for the most part, thanks to the work of Don Pedro José de Meneces, fourth Marquis of Marialva (1713-99), cavalry general and head rider of the Alter de Chao stud, in the province of Alentejo. This remarkable rider achieved the fusion of traditional bullfighting riding and the newer equitation teachings coming from France, the supporters of which were fiercely opposed. The shoulder-in and releasing of contact held no secrets for him. He mastered his art as finely as La Guérinière and his riding presented an indisputable affinity in both style and spirit with the French system, since the emphasis was placed on the art, the brilliance of the presentation and the perfection of the execution.

Although a long period separates 1807 and 1979, the equestrian art was maintained in its most vivid form, in part thanks to bullfighting on horseback.

A national form of entertainment enjoyed by the public besides being cultivated by monarchs and aristocrats, bullfighting allowed for the conservation of the same work methods and the same types of horses as well as a dressage and a manoeuvrability that are not ends in themselves but rather a beginning, necessary for winning the fight whilst protecting the mount (and its rider!) from any harm.

One of the most notable aspects of this School and its stud is that they represent an exceptional human adventure. Indeed, having almost no resources at their disposal, they were both the result of exemplary tenacity and relentless work!

The Alter Real breed
is stabilising itself
once more within the
national Alter Stud.
Five or six young
horses are allocated
each year to the
School after having
been broken in.

First, the Alter stud, where Alter Real horses come from, was founded in 1748, during the reign of Don Joâo, following Prince Don José's impetus. Serving a national purpose, this stud is said to have originally had a herd of almost fifty Andalusian broodmares[2], although more recent sources mention up to three hundred mares. Up until 1801, the Alter stud prospered, in particular under the reign of D. José I (1750-77) who granted it generous funds and increased the number of its broodmares and stallions considerably. The Alter Real was the only breed there at the time, with mares from other breeds only serving to produce mules. Selected and trained by the greatest master riders (including the Marquis of Marialva), the Alter Real horse made the Portuguese Court famous and took part, amongst others, in many Haute École performances at the Royal Manège in Belém. But in the early part of the nineteenth century, the stud was requisitioned during the Napoleonic campaigns. The Alter Real horse was then mixed with French mares captured at the Battle of Salamanca (1812) and then, later, with mares coming from the cavalry regiment auctions. In 1828 it was once more crossed with Arab and Moroccan stallions to create a breed of fast riding and driving horses. A long period of decline began then, during which the breed was slowly dying out. In 1938, the last two stallions which remained useable thanks to the purity of their bloodlines were sold at auction. The Alter Real horse could then have disappeared completely. Thankfully, these two specimens were bought back by Dr Ruy de Andrade, a great Portuguese celebrity, who then handed them over to the Breeding Services' General Management. In 1942, from these two stallions and eleven broodmares, through selection and patience, the reconstruction of the Alter Real breed was undertaken. Although the idea to restore Real Picaria was, without a doubt, a collegial idea, Dr Ruy de Andrade was, if not at its origin, an essential agent for this change. For him, and for the master riders involved in the venture, recreating the academy was more than the simple reconstruction of a school lost in the ups and downs of history. It was a whole page of Portugal's history during which – through many exchanges, particularly since the sixteenth century – a technique was developed, which was first vital for the war horse, before becoming majestic for court horses. This complex technique is the essential element for the perfection of the art. As a social symbol, but also a means for personal elevation, it was held in high esteem by kings.

However, at the start, in 1979, the School had no premises for training. The four master riders constituting the School – Dr Guilherme Borba (who later became its head rider and who was, several years previously, technical director of the Spanish School of Jerez), José d'Athayde (who was a rider at the Alter Stud and a torero on horseback), Filipe Graciosa (head rider since 1986) and Francisco Cancelle de Abreu – each kept their horse (four horses for four master riders) at home and graciously rode them after their day's work. All were students of Nuno Oliveira, already considered to be the "great equestrian intellect of the twentieth century" and a master of the same calibre as La Guérinière or Marialva. The horses were thus being worked by very high quality master

Above
The red velvet frock
coat and the tricorn
hat make up the
basics of the
gala uniform.
The "Portuguese"
plait is a double braid
created using two
wide silk ribbons.

Opposite
The stirrups are
struck with the
Portuguese arms.

Above
Flatwork on the
long reins is an
exercise used
by the four
Schools; here
an aspiring
rider.

Opposite
Riders loosen
their horses up in
the magnificent
gardens of the
Queluz Palace.

riders and with a desire for perfection which still remains at the heart of the School. They met once a month at the manège of Fonte Boa to harmonise the progress of the group and set the movements to music. Proof of their incredible work, these four master riders performed their first demonstration at the Paris Horse Show in December of that very same year. In 1980, the School gave its second gala in The Hague, Netherlands. A great turning point came in 1981. Cancella de Abreau left the School and was replaced by João Pedro Rodriguez. Henceforth, the training took place at the Portuguese Equestrian Society in Lisbon, and highly talented riders, who later become quasi-mythical, joined the ranks: Luis Valença Rodrigues, Antonio Borba Monteiro and João Trigueiros de Aragão. Within a few years, the School built both an international reputation and an international dimension. It regularly performed abroad, notably in England, upon invitation of the Queen in 1986 and in front of President Reagan.

The number of horses increased (twenty-five horses in 1985) as well as the number of riders, up until 1996, the year during which the School definitively became established in Queen D. Amélia's stables, rebuilt in the gardens of the Queluz Palace. It is there that, every morning, it is now possible to watch the horses and master riders in training as well as attend weekly performances.

Placed under the aegis of the Ministry of Agriculture[3] which covered all of its financing, it became a Foundation in 2007, funded half by the State and half by private companies. This Foundation combines the School and the Alter stud. It is responsible for

I T IS RESPONSIBLE FOR THE CONSERVATION AND PROMOTION OF PORTUGUESE EQUESTRIAN HERITAGE, FOR PRACTISING, DIVULGING AND TEACHING TRADITIONAL EQUESTRIAN ART, FOR PERPETUATING AND DEVELOPING THE BREEDING OF ALTER REAL HORSES.

the conservation and promotion of Portuguese equestrian heritage, for practising, divulging and teaching traditional equestrian art and for perpetuating and developing the breeding of Alter Real horses. With approximately fifteen master riders and about sixty horses, the School is ready to take on any challenge, including picking up the thread of equestrian tradition: to return to the Royal Manège of Belém, in Lisbon, which today houses the carriage museum. It was in this arena, built in 1786 (on the site of an earlier arena built in 1726 by King João V) at the instigation of Infante D. João, later João VI, son of Maria I and Pedro III and an equestrian art enthusiast, that the Alter horses used to be trained and presented and where they experienced their finest hour.

**The riders**

In Lisbon, the appointment of the head rider and of the director is not standardised. At present, Filipe Graciosa concurrently fills the positions of head rider (since 1986) and of director (since 2000). His appointment was a reflection of his numerous qualities.[4]

Opposite
The elegance of the
pesade. In order to
maintain perfect
balance, the horse
must not be subjected
to any constraint.

As in Vienna and in Jerez, the Portuguese School recruits its riders (a total of approximately fifteen) from amongst young people and trains them in full. The transmission of knowledge is "filial", taking the form of an apprenticeship, where the master teaches everything to his student. It is the head rider and the "veteran master riders" who decide upon the acceptance of candidates and who monitor their training. The students are taken on for three years in order to learn about horses and riding and to verify their skills and aptitude for the job. They are only accepted into the School if the School needs them. Depending on their competence and their results, they become aspiring riders (Aspirantes), deputy riders (Picadores Ajudantes), riders (Picadores) and then master riders (Mestres Picadores).

The master riders' uniform takes its inspiration from the eighteenth century. It was designed by José António Torcato Freitas. After multiple sketches and meetings with Mr Fernando d'Andrade, the School founder, and his collaborators, it was decided that the uniform would be burgundy.

The gala uniform consists of a long burgundy velvet frock coat falling to the knee and worn open at the front. It features a black collar, black and gold stripes, two big pockets and large golden buttons bearing the arms of King D. João V. Under the coat, the master rider wears a relatively long white silk waistcoat with two pockets on either side and fitted in the back thanks to two fabric fastenings. The shirt is white, collarless, with French cuffs and cufflinks. With it is worn a white stock, crossed at the front and tucked under the waistcoat so that the waistcoat's top button

is visible. The hat is a black felt tricorn with black and gold stripes around the rim and, on the left, a red and white ribbon with gold buttons bearing the arms of King D. João V. Head riders wear a golden escutcheon on the left.

The gloves are white leather. The breeches are cream coloured. Their waist is high and tightened over the thigh thanks to four buttons above the knee. They no longer possess an opening on the side of the thigh, as they did in the eighteenth century, since today's elasticated fabrics make them easy to put on. The socks are white silk and cover the knee. The boots are black leather jodhpur boots and are worn with long gaiters that open in a V at the front of the knee, tightened at the side in an olive branch pattern. The spurs are yellow metal, tied to a thick leather strap that passes over the top of the foot and is fastened with a buckle on the outside of the foot. The whip is a quince tree branch. The work uniform is the same as that for galas, but without the burgundy velvet frock coat. In winter, the white waistcoat is replaced with a burgundy velvet one, decorated with black and gold stripes and golden buttons. Then the master riders wear the traditional Portuguese coat with the fox collar, known as a capote à alentejana. In summer, the master riders ride in their

Previous double page
The bits are stamped
with the Portuguese
arms.

Opposite
Rider in pesade
in the gardens
of the Queluz
Palace, Lisbon.

waistcoats, the sleeves of the shirts thus being visible. They can wear a black raincoat bearing the School's crest. The students wear a burgundy, v-necked pullover over a shirt with a burgundy and blue striped collar. Lastly, the grooms have a dark blue uniform with a large cap and wear overalls for cleaning the stables.

**The horses**

The Portuguese School has approximately sixty Alter Real horses, all stallions. The Alter Real is the "historical" horse presented at the king's court in Portugal. Although it is now stabilised again, it is not officially considered a breed in its own right. It descends from the purebred Lusitano. "According to Bernardo Lima, who was the first Portuguese zootechnician, the Alter Real horse is a 'horse whose head is slightly square (forehead), fine, slightly convex from the base of the forehead to the tip of the nose, joined to a beautiful and elegant neck, attached to a well proportioned trunk with prominent withers, a slightly concave back, wide breast, flanks almost round, normal belly, large, muscular and gently sloping hindquarters, ending in a thick tail bearing much hair. The body is supported by four strong legs (the hind legs being slightly under) that are well muscled in the upper part, but fine and well defined from the knee and hock to the ground, erring slightly through a lack of length of the forearm and an excess in that of the cannon bone, which facilitates school airs and elevated paces but hinders speed in racing. Courage, power and elegance of a noble lightness, a little playful without being skittish', here

T HE PORTUGUESE SCHOOL'S TACK AND ACCESSORIES ARE IDENTICAL REPLICAS OF THOSE USED AT THE KING'S COURT.

is, all in all, what was and still is the good Andalusian horse (almost, if not completely free of Germanic blood) and also the good Alter Real horse, the best horses of the fine Celto-Iberian or Betico-Lusitano types of breeds (in *Archivo Rural*, 1664) ."[5]

Measuring about 16 hands, exclusively bay, elegant and athletic with a lively temperament and a reputation for high intelligence, keen, brave, very sensitive, used for all types of riding, it is therefore particularly gifted for Haute École, especially thanks to the elegant and elevated movements of its forelegs. It is bred at the Alter stud, whose primary aim, other than the preservation and maintenance of the breed, is to supply the School (which is why the Foundation created in 2007 combines the School and the Alter stud). About fifteen young horses are broken in each year before joining the School at about four years of age. Out of these fifteen, the School only keeps the best, i.e. about five or six horses.

The Portuguese School's tack and accessories are identical replicas of those used at the king's court. The "Relvas" style saddle is used for daily work. Of natural colour, it is made from highly supple leather and has a relatively low cantle and pommel. The seat is elaborately worked, while thick veining is etched

The Schools
of Lisbon, Jerez
and Vienna are
linked to a very
identifiable breed
of horse. The Alter
Real is keen, brave,
generous and
predestined for
the airs above
the ground.

on the saddle flaps. The presentation and gala saddle is a classical Portuguese saddle identical to those used for bullfighting. In the same colour as the aforementioned saddle, it has high "battes" at the front and the back. These two saddles are beautifully decorated with silver tacks and both bear the coat of arms of King João V on the bottom of the rear part of the saddle flaps.

The tread of the stirrup is circular. The branches of the stirrups are relatively big and are all stamped with the Portuguese arms. When the horse is worked in hand or on the long reins, the stirrups are attached on either side of the cantle using fine leather straps, whose buckles are also finely worked. The saddles are held in place with a crupper and a breastplate at the centre of which the king's arms can be seen once more. Behind both saddles, a small, aesthetically pleasing, badger-fur rug preserves the rider's jacket from staining by the horse's sweat.

The horses are ridden in a snaffle or a double bridle. Both are in natural coloured leather and have buckles and loops made from finely worked golden metal. The shanks of the bit are stamped with the Portuguese arms. For work on the long reins, the horses wear a burgundy velvet saddle cloth with wide golden edging and the Portuguese arms embroidered in gold on either side. During daily work and training sessions, the horses are ridden with free manes and tails. However, during shows, the mane is plaited in the Portuguese style – a double plait made with wide yellow and white silk ribbons. This plaiting is done using a needle and requires great mastery.

Opposite
The head rider
and his stallion,
in passage, in the
Queluz Palace
gardens.

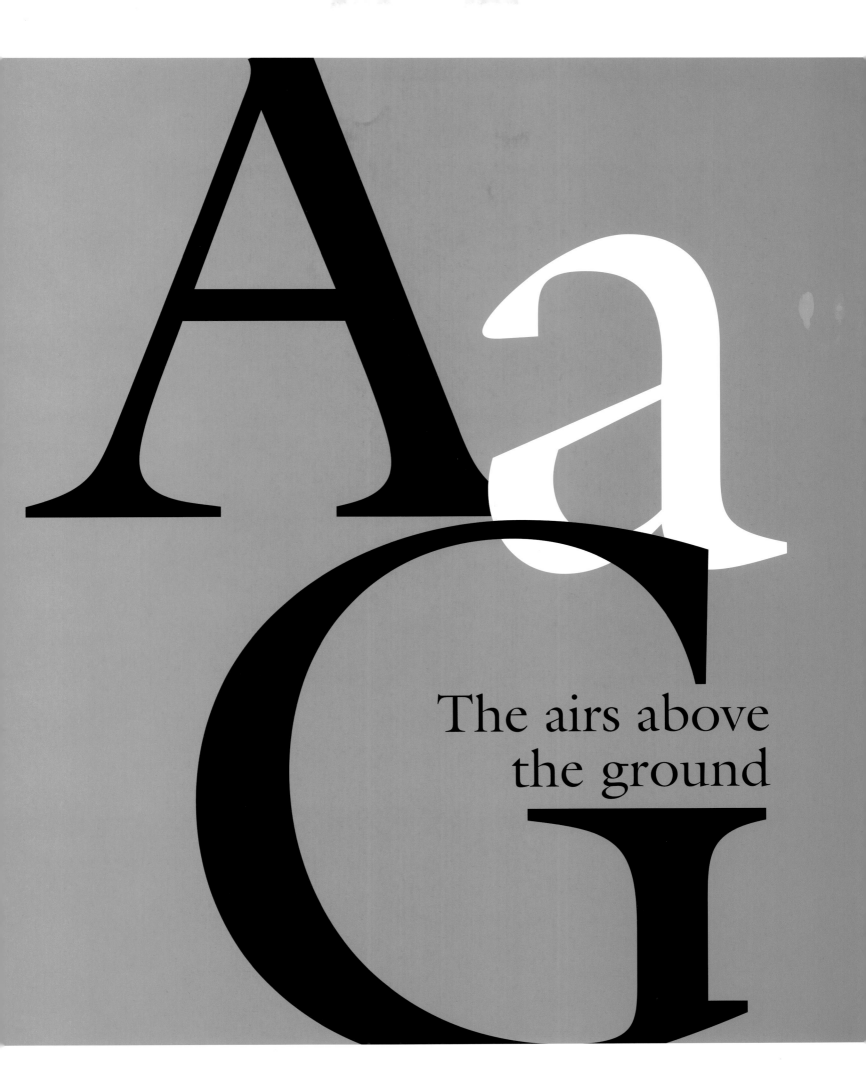

The airs above
the ground

Above
In the pesade,
the horse must
maintain balanced
immobility for a
few moments.

The origin of the airs above the ground is still the subject of debate. Some think they served a purpose in battle, others not. Thus, the croupade, for example, would not be a buck aimed to push the enemy away. In the only book specifically written on the subject, Jean-Claude Barry writes, "to be convinced, one needs only practise them. When one knows the preparation and the precision they require, it is difficult to imagine executing them in the middle of a confrontation where speed and prompt reactions are vital and where any involuntary or imprecise action from the rider could be interpreted by the horse. Furthermore, the weight of the tack as well as that of the rider in armour were a handicap for the charger and limited its agility."[1] This is confirmed by many other authors such as Gaspard de Saunier in *The art of cavalry* (1756): "While the horse is rearing to perform a courbette, the enemy would take advantage of the moment, by reaching its hindquarters, to overcome the rider, or kill him, with no risk." Nonetheless, maybe a croupade – a good kick! – at the heart of combat, saved the lives of a few soldiers…

Appearing during the Renaissance, the airs above the ground are thought to have had three purposes: to enhance the final part of carousels, to allow the rider to prove his stability, lightness and merit in the saddle and to represent the culmination of a school horse's training. Galas having replaced carousels, the school jumps indisputably fulfil these three aims.

As we have seen, the emergence of firearms on the battlefield profoundly altered war strategy in the fifteenth century. Horses needed to be better trained and to respond better to their riders. If the aim of the school airs was to obtain perfect submission and great manoeuvrability from the battle horse, the airs above the ground proved the rider's perfect steadiness in the saddle and reinforced the schooling. "Pirouettes and half pirouettes allow for quicker turning around in combat. And although the airs above the ground do not have such an advantage, they present that of giving the horse the lightness required to clear ditches and hedges, which contributes to the safety and security of the rider."[2]

Up until the eighteenth century, a profusion of airs above the ground existed, some of them quite fantastical. François Robichon de La Guérinière classified and ordered them and gave them a concrete theoretical basis. In his book *École de cavalerie* (1733), he thus distinguishes the airs from the airs above the ground. Airs are movements performed close to the ground, such as passage, piaffer, gallopade, changing the rein, circles, half circles, passade, pirouette and terre-a-terre.[3] The airs above the ground are those where the horse leaves the ground. La Guérinière counted seven of them: the pesade, the mezair, the courbette, the croupade, the ballotade , the capriole and the pas-et-le-saut.[4]

Although standardised, these airs did not remain fixed. Each school made them evolve and adapted them according to its own style and history. Today, only the capriole – the height of dressage – remains the same movement in all four schools. During shows, the audience can enjoy several airs, performed with their specific characteristics by horses in hand,

Overleaf
The courbette,
as it is practised
in Saumur.

or ridden: the pesade, the levade, the courbette, the croupade and the capriole. Vienna presents the levade, the courbette, the capriole and the "old" capriole. The Cadre Noir presents the latter three. Jerez presents the pesade, the capriole, the courbette and the Viennese levade but also the "old" courbette. Lisbon presents the levade and the capriole.

## The levade

The levade comes from the pesade (César Fiaschi named it orsade, as the horse seemed to rear up like a bear). It is performed (for the public) in Vienna, Jerez and Lisbon in an almost identical way, the height of the forelimbs varying depending on the horse and not on the school. In a way, it constitutes an introduction to the airs above the ground. Its name comes from *posato*, a sixteenth century Italian word which means "to rest", "to lean on", as the horse bends its haunches, seeming to sit down, "resting on" its hindquarters, before lightly elevating its forehand whilst bending its front legs. Until the nineteenth century, the horse's body had to maintain a forty-five degree angle with the ground. Today however, pesade designates a movement in which this angle (and therefore the elevation of the forehand) is over forty-five degrees, while the movement is known as a levade when the angle is less. In both cases, the horse must remain immobile for a moment.

Like all the airs above the ground, it is first taught in hand. The handler initially asks for an energetic piaffer, which he gradually shortens. By acting with his whip under the hocks, he causes increased engagement of the hind legs while exerting slight tensions with his driving rein, which finally leads to the execution of the movement. Once it is has been learnt in hand, it is taught with the added weight of the rider. The movement is always asked for from a piaffer by intensifying the leg action and by placing the hands a little higher than normal to tell the horse that it will have to lift its forehand. The extraordinary difficulty of this movement comes from the strength and flexibility the horse needs to "sit" in this way, but also from the requirement to teach the horse, once balanced, to keep the posture and wait for its rider's instructions before allowing its forelegs to return to the ground. When instructed by the rider, the horse must not return heavily to the ground, but, on the contrary, it must "alight" with grace and softness. For the master rider, it is important not only to allow the horse to perform the air of its own accord, but also not to disturb its execution. The rider thus remains "sitting quietly", the upper body neither forward – which would overload the forehand and would risk unbalancing the horse – nor backward – which would overload the hindquarters and would result in excessive strain for the horse, or could lead to it stepping back – endeavouring not to hinder the horse's balance.

## The croupade

The word croupade comes from the old French *groupade* which means "to catch" and the Italian *gropatta* which means "to gather". Originally, the horse would leap into the air and, whilst horizontal, gather its hind legs under its body by placing them at the same height as its forelegs.

Vienna still performs this movement in shows, unlike the Cadre Noir. Indeed, Saumur performs three airs above the ground, inherited from Mr Codier, first head rider of the School of Cavalry in 1825. Although its capriole is similar to that of the other schools, its courbette and croupade are unique. In the Saumur croupade, the horse leans on its forelegs, lifts its hindquarters and performs an energetic buck, whilst staying on the bit. Very different from the Versailles concept, it gained a specific style at the Cadre Noir (following the example of the courbette) for several reasons. These reasons include the expansion, in the nineteenth century, of a military, then sporting type of riding, Cordier's own interpretation of the movement (he had greatly simplified its definition), then the Count d'Aure's and finally, the horses who, having been Iberian at the start of the Manège (therefore having great propensity for collection) were replaced during the nineteenth century with French and English breeds, better adapted for military riding but with more limited physical abilities (especially in the lowering of the haunches).

## The courbette

The word courbette comes from the sixteenth century Italian word *corvetta*, which means "to curve". Originally it was an extension of the mezair (itself sometimes called the half-courbette, intermediary gait between the terre-a-terre and the courbette, in which the horse takes balanced steps forward whilst lifting its forehand): in essence, the horse flexes its hindquarters and performs a small jump with its hindlegs. In the courbette, the horse lifts its forehand further. It is therefore a more sustained and even more balanced air than the mezair, in which the highly flexed hindquarters accompany the forelegs as they return to the ground. At the end of a series of courbettes, it was customary to perform the last one very high and stationary.

Jerez performs a courbette which is undoubtedly the closest to the classical movement, Vienna and the Cadre Noir having moved away from it. In Vienna, the movement varies essentially from the old exercise in that the forehand no longer touches the ground between leaps. This unique feature, developed during the second half of the nineteenth century, renders this school jump much more spectacular, but also much more difficult.

At the Cadre Noir, the courbette is an inverse movement to the croupade: the horse lifts itself up onto its hind legs, hocks slightly bent, forelegs bent – a sort of rear on command.

## The capriole

The word capriole, or cabriole, comes from the sixteenth century Italian word *caprio* which describes the jump of a goat, or more precisely that of kid. In the movement, considered by La Guérinière to be "the most elevated and the most perfect of all the jumps", the horse leaps above the ground and, at the highest point of its jump, performs the most violent kick possible.

Practised by the four schools, and the culmination of the horse's education, it requires numerous physical attributes (suppleness, musculature, strength, energy) but also psychological qualities.

Opposite
A ridden capriole,
taken just before
the horse kicks
its hind legs.

Above
The levade is
traditionally lower
than the pesade.

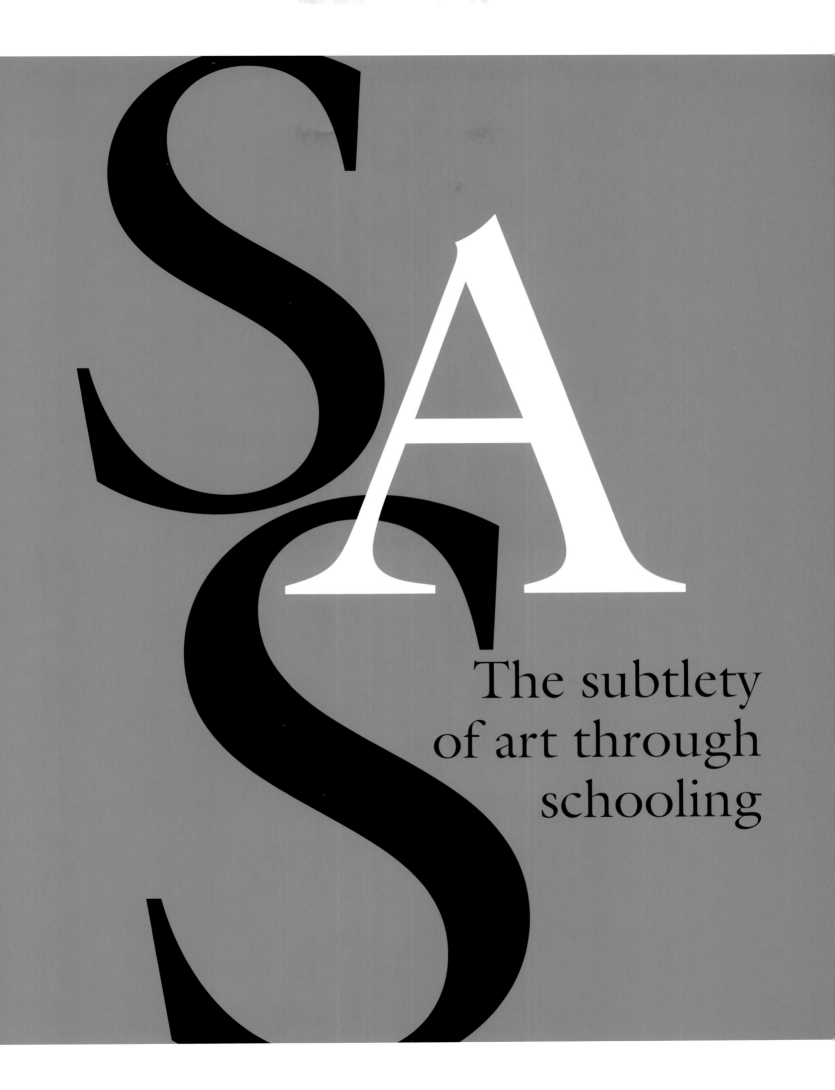

The subtlety
of art through
schooling

The four schools have a common equestrian heritage coming from the Renaissance and in particular from the works of François Robichon de La Guérinière, considered to be "the" great master of the eighteenth century. Through him, during his time, both theory and practice reached an unprecedented level of coherence through a coding of "the rules of the art". The excellence of his work not only allowed horses to "give" their best whilst perfectly maintaining their physical and mental qualities, but also to guarantee that they completely fulfilled the purpose for which they were destined.

Despite having common roots, these four schools' riding techniques and their shows display similarities and differences beyond those of the uniforms and horse breeds. It would be a mistake to think that they apply the same equitation or that they present similar work.

Devised in the nineteenth century for Vienna, Saumur and to some extent Lisbon, and from the seventeenth century for Jerez,[1] these presentations, "devised rather than re-created"[2] – that only reveal a part of each school's work – can be divided into three types of scenes: group movements, individual presentations, and a sort of mixture of the two with a heavier cultural distinction. The group arrangements are principally based upon the synchronisation of movements and the alignment of riders. The Cadre Noir jumpers' courbettes performed at the command of the head rider, the diagonals in half-pass at Saumur, Vienna or Lisbon in their respective carousels, or the perfectly synchronous pirouettes in canter of the eight Doma Vaquera riders of Jerez are some of their highlights. They all have a strong national identity: the Saumur carousel is of military tradition and proves its worth in the symmetry of the ensemble and the perfect lightness of the execution (symbol of the French school). That of Vienna is reminiscent of a ballet. The utilitarian equitation of Lisbon and Jerez are very identifiable, and the women sitting behind the saddle are typical of the férias of Jerez.

The individual presentations (solos, pas de deux or trios, in hand or ridden) always bring the perfection of a horse's dressage, or the exceptional qualities of a horse-rider pairing, to the fore. They are usually of a much higher technical level than the group presentations, such as, for example, the long rein solo of a Viennese master rider (at Paris-Bercy in November 2007) who linked about fifty-one tempi changes on a figure of eight whilst maintaining unaltered cadence and rigour from start to finish. They present the major difficulties of classical dressage, difficulties which the four schools have in common. Finally, certain scenes present a sort of mixture of the two, culturally very identifiable, where several master riders take it in turn to present their work. This is the case, for example, with the Saumur master riders who jump over a table at which other riders are sat dining, as it was done during the Belle Époque.

Previous page facing
Start of the
Portuguese
School's carousel.

Above
The head rider of
the Cadre Noir
presents his horse
in school walk.

Although all four schools follow La Guérinière, there are numerous differences in principles, doctrine, means and methods which are within the grasp of an inexperienced audience. As well as the break in the continuity of the transmission (such as in Saumur, Lisbon and Jerez), or the modification of certain facets of the tradition, each school has had its own interpre-tation of La Guérinière depending on their culture and their requirements. Even at the School in Vienna, where the transmission could be considered the purest, classical dressage has seen some adjustments.

During a conference given at the 11th symposium of the École Nationale d'Équitation, Karl Kristen von Steten[3] perfectly demonstrated, for example, how the use of the double bridle, the lift of the neck and the bend advocated by von Hünersdorf, a master rider who ranks amongst the great "classical" references of Vienna, modified La Guérinière's principles, and what this changed in terms of balance and lightness. Moreover, Vienna states that its work is based on La Guérinière's book, but also on the works of Max von Weyrother, of Louis Seeger (1799 – c. 1860), of Baron von Oeynhausen (1812–1875) and on von Holbein's[4] directives, which somewhat clarified or modified their principles.

As much in Lisbon as in Jerez, utilitarian equitation and bullfighting have strongly influenced the collective subconscious and, in a way, modified the so-called "classical" approach. Louis Fabre[5] points out that "bullfighting requires certain 'moral' qualities on the part of the horse, such as a fine response to the aids, trusting submission and adhesion to a common strategy. It equally requires physical qualities such as mobility in all directions, that is to say laterally, thanks to their lateral exercises and transitions, but also longitudinally thanks to their incredible bursts of speed, their harsh braking, even their sudden halts and, here again, all their transitions. It therefore requires the capacity to shift the balance from the hindquarters to the forehand and vice-versa. It is precisely through this inversion, that is to say the shift onto its hindquarters, that the horse must ensure that it carries its weight in preparation for a new and imminent propulsion. This propulsion can only happen at such speed via the equality of the bend in the hips, the stifles, and the hocks in the collection". Thus, in Portugal, he confirms, "academic equitation has generally maintained this athletic and aesthetic necessity of the equal bend of the hind legs' joints which is, evidently, thanks to the omnipresence of bullfighting in the equestrian tradition of this country. [...] That is why, what remains of the Old Portuguese School in today's School, is the pursuit of mobility, both physical and mental, of both riders and horses, in an atmosphere that is both artistic and military, or rather combative." This mobility finds one of its expressions (for example) in the multipli-cation of transitions, both longitudinal and lateral, as Carlos Andrade[6] advocated in his time, having himself borrowed them from Newcastle, and not La Guérinière.

Although it is reasonable to think that working equitation and bullfighting influenced the Haute École riding in Jerez, constant participation in high level dressage competitions in which the Spanish master riders excel brilliantly has also unquestionably influenced their present practices. Indeed, the complexity of the dressage tests and the rapid sequence of movements in international competitions, require direction and tension on the part of the horse – both "physically" in its top line and "mentally" in its reactivity to the aids – specific to this discipline. Beyond the squabbles regarding "lightness" between their respective partisans, bullfighting, competition dressage or classical dressage each possess different aims which have shaped the School's riding style and conditioned its search for horses. As for the Cadre Noir, it has shone in an outdoor style of riding since the middle of the nineteenth century (racing and endurance in the nineteenth century, show jumping and eventing competitions since the twentieth century) which can only have influenced its equitation. Jean-Pierre Tuloup, one of its past master riders, writes that Saumur has achieved "this long dreamt of alliance between scholarly riding and bold riding".[7] The characteristics of their mounts undoubtedly corroborate this assertion, as although the Cadre Noir horses possess, a more horizontal balance and a mindset predisposing them to "racing" and jumping (domains in which they excel), and although they do not have the mental and physical propensity for collection of the Iberian horses, they nevertheless also achieve the piaffer and airs above the ground (movements which do require collection).

Although these divergences and unique features remain to be studied in more depth, one can argue that the four schools are not "academies" with similar equitation. They practise and transmit a heritage which they never cease to enrich, each in their own way. Despite sharing common principles and presenting well defined airs (passage, piaffer, changing of the rein, circles, half circles, pirouette, terre-a-terre, successive flying changes up to tempi changes), they maintain differences in their methods and their implementation, which modify their results. But should one compare Baudelaire to Rimbaud? Or Mozart to Beethoven? Beyond all these distinctions (horse breeds, uniforms, settings, etc.) "a feeble understanding of the rules does not forbid the admiring of the result":[8] they all succeed in making the horse sublime and in "perfecting nature through the subtlety of art",[9] which is what gives them their splendour.

## Bercy 2007

Some of the schools had already given shared performances. In 1972 for example, Vienna had invited the Cadre Noir to commemorate its 400 years of existence whilst the Cadre Noir had already invited the schools of Lisbon (in 2003) and of Jerez (in 2004) for the Printemps des Écuyers. Similarly, Jerez had invited the three other schools to Seville for the 25th anniversary of its existence. But the four schools had never performed together in grand formation. The show which united them in November 2007 was therefore an exceptional event. Initiated by the Cadre Noir, it was also made possible thanks to the professional and friendly links that the riders have been forming with each other for a very long time. Beyond the technical constraints (designing and organising the event over many months, then housing, feeding and training sixty riders and eighty horses, with sometimes very different paces of life, a unique

Above
For almost twenty
years, the École
Nationale d'Équitation
has owned a few
foreign horses.
Some Lusitanos
have left a particular
mark during their
career, particularly
on the long reins
(Verdi pictured
here).

Since 1984, the
Cadre Noir in Saumur
has welcomed a few
women. This is one
of the many signs
of the opening up
of the School.

show had to be created in which each school could demonstrate its talent and uniqueness, whilst all the while being part of a coherent ensemble. With 15,000 spectators per night and three shows with the whole audience on their feet, the Sipas (the organisers) and the four temples of classical dressage gave the audience (45,000 people in total), both together and individually, a multitude of breathtaking moments, filled with emotion, which will remain etched in memories for a long time to come.

**Tradition and progress**

This brief glimpse into the four temples of Haute École, the Spanish Riding School in Vienna, the Cadre Noir in Saumur, the Portuguese School of Equestrian Art in Lisbon and the Royal Andalusian School of Equestrian Art in Jerez, tends to reveal three profiles. An equestrian university in Saumur, a sort of Silicon Valley of equitation,[10] at the peak of high-level sport, teaching and modernity.

Two equestrian academies (Vienna and Lisbon) of traditional style,[11] where so-called classical riding is practised and taught from an Haute École angle within the cultural nuances specific to each country.

In both these academies, the horses used are specific and linked to their particular histories. Finally, an Andalusian cultural centre in Jerez, which, based on equestrian tradition,progressively embraces all aspects of Andalusian culture relating to it.

Their common presentation at Paris-Bercy in November 2007 was an opportunity to remember how each of them is a true gift for our times. Indeed, in a period where the principles of equestrian art are being diluted into "sporting and leisure" types of riding, with declining standards, they give us, together and separately, and beyond their particular histories, a continuum of discipline, rigour, precision and tradition, at the service of an ideal, the beauty, expression and living timelessness which bears two names: collection and lightness. Drawing their principles right at the source of "ancient equitation", these four great schools are a testament to the fact that the poetry of riding, in its most free and accomplished form, can only find its true expression through work and method. They also demonstrate that the present can only be illuminated by shedding light on its past, or, in other words, that it is by feeding them at the roots of their history that the flowers of the future can bloom.

The Paris-Bercy show
in November 2007 was
an event which will remain
in the history books.
It was the first time that
these four Schools had
performed together. It was
an opportunity for multiple
exchanges between the
riders and the formation
of numerous friendships.

# Glossary

**Airs.** The airs are movements executed on the ground. La Guérinière defined the passage, the piaffer, the gallopade, the change of rein, the circle, the semi-circle, the passade, the pirouette and the terre-a-terre as such.

**Airs above the ground.** These are the airs in which the horse leaves the ground. For La Guérinière, they encompassed the pesade, the mezair, the courbette, the croupade, the ballotade, the capriole and the pas-et-le-saut.

**Ballotade.** From the sixteenth century Italian *balzare*, to jump, and *balsatto*, which means little leap. The ballotade is a school jump in which the horse jumps horizontally and frees its hind legs, as though it wanted to kick, but without fully extending them. It prepares the horse for the capriole, without necessarily being a required step, especially if the horse has a natural aptitude for the school jumps.

**Capriole/Cabriole.** A school jump from the sixteenth century Italian *caprio*, which means goat's leap, by analogy with the way a kid jumps, in which the horse jumps horizontally then bucks.

**Collection.** The state in which the horse is completely balanced, able to make full use of its mass. A state from which the extension of a gait is as easy to obtain as its shortening.

**Courbette.** An air above the ground in which the horse lifts its forehand.

**Croupade** (ancient). An air above the ground in which the horse jumps up, gathers its legs under its body and keeps them flexed.

**Flying change.** The horse, just like dogs or cats, canters by placing its legs in a particular order when moving to the left (called canter on the left leg) and in a different order when moving to the right (called canter on the right leg). Changing from the canter on the left leg to the canter on the right leg, or vice-versa, whilst remaining in canter, is called a flying change, and resembles the little jumps of a skipping child.

**Gallopade.** The gallopade is one of the airs and describes a very shortened school canter, in which the horse's hindquarters remain diligent, active, which gives an effect of suppleness, of flexibility and of grace which is highly prized, particularly so in the carousels of old.

**Haute École.** A horse's work is broadly divided into three phases. Breaking-in the horse aims to get it to accept (and understand) the bit and the bridle. The Basse École intends to "restore, whilst under the saddle, the grace of posture and movement it naturally has in the wild and that are altered by the weight and actions of the rider". 1 Haute École seeks to stylise its gaits and to "perfect nature via the subtlety of art". 2 Passage and piaffer, for example, are Haute École airs.

**Mezair.** The mezair, sometimes called half-courbette, come from the Italian *mezzo* which means "in the middle". It is an intermediate gait between the terre-a-terre and the courbette in which the horse is more and more symmetrical, increasingly lifting its forehand and moving in a focussed way. The horse bends its hind legs and performs a little leap with its forelegs.

**Pas-et-le-saut.** The seventh air above the ground defined by La Guérinière, in which the horse links a shortened canter to a terre-a-terre, performs a courbette, then a capriole and so on.

**Passade.** The passade is an air that is close to the ground in which the horse is ridden along the same length of track, changing at each end, from right to left and left to right, passing again and again over the same line. It can be performed in collected canter or at a gallop.

**Passage.** Sometimes called passège, from the Italian word *spassegio*, which means a stroll, the passage is a very slow trot, in which the period of suspension is maximal. The horse looks as though it is dancing in this air, sometimes also known as "parade trot".

**Pesade.** An air above the ground in which the horse sits on its hindquarters and lifts its forehand, its forelegs bent. It is the height of the collection and education of a school horse.

**Piaffer.** A sort of stationary trot in which the horse has to flex its hindquarters and to strongly collect itself. The piaffer is one of the Haute École airs and can only be attempted with a highly trained horse.

**Pirouette.** A movement performed in walk or canter in which the horse pivots around its hind legs.

**Terre-a-terre.** The terre-a-terre is a two-beat canter in which the horse appears to be executing small leaps from its forelegs to its hind legs and vice-versa. It usually serves as a foundation for the airs above the ground because these are also performed in two beats.

To discover the four schools:

**The Spanish Riding School in Vienna**
http://www.spanische-reitschule.com

**The Cadre Noir in Saumur**
http://www.cadrenoir.fr

**The Portuguese School
of Equestrian Art in Lisbon**
http://www.snc.min-agricultura.pt/epae/
http://www.cavalonet.com/epae

**The Royal Andalusian School
of Equestrian Art in Jerez**
http://www.realescuela.org

# Notes

## Introduction

**1** Contrary to the French and Italian knights who, at the time, rode with four reins.

**2** The rectangle formed by the four hooves on the ground.

## From Grisone to La Guérinière

**1** Circa 430BC to circa 355BC. He was the author of an important written body of work, including *The art of horsemanship*, still considered a remarkable book today.

**2** His treatise appeared in 1550. He achieved great success and was translated in most European languages during that century.

**3** Veterinary and anatomical knowledge of the horse.

**4** See the chapter on the airs above the ground.

**5** Yves Grange, (1981), *Le cheval oublié, essai sur les aspects socio-politiques de la relation de l'homme et du cheval en France (1614-1914) [The forgotten horse, essay on the socio-political aspects of the relation between man and horse in France (1614-1914)]*, doctoral thesis in administrative sociology, Institute for political studies, Grenoble.

**6** The expression is borrowed from Étienne Saurel, (1971), *Histoire de l'équitation [History of equitation]*, Stock.

**7** *Trésorier de France* in Alençon.

**8** Gérard Guillotel, (2000, July 14) in: *Essai de reviviscence de l'écuyer F R. de la Guérinière et de ses proches [Essay of revification of the rider F R. de la Guérinière and of his contemporaries]*, ENE Symposium, Belin, 2000.

**9** Marie Auriol-Jollinier, (2000, July 14) in: *La Guérinière, premier pédagogue équestre moderne [La Guérinière, first modern equestrian educationalist]*, ENE Symposium, Belin, 2000.

**10** André Monteilhet, (1979), *Les maîtres de l'œuvre équestre [The masters of equestrian work]*, Odège.

**11** The Duke of Newcastle, British horseman, 1592 – 1676.

**12** F. Robichon de La Guérinière, (1729), *École de cavalerie [School of horsemanship]*.

**13** *Ibidem*.

**14** Henry Wynalmen, in: Sylvia Loch, (1994), *Histoire de l'équitation classique [The history of classical equitation]*, Maloine.

## The Spanish Riding School in Vienna

**1** Löhneyssen

**2** After 1918 and the collapse of the Austro-Hungarian monarchy, it was the Piber stud, in Styria, which provided the School's horses.

**3** Hans Handler, Erich Lessing, (1972), *La Haute École Espagnole de Vienne [The Spanish riding school of Vienna]*, Albin Michel.

**4** Who returned them after the War.

**5** A special law to this effect (*Spanische Hofreitschule Gesetz, BGBl. 1, N°115, 24 November 2000*) was voted for in Parliament, to give it legal status.

**6** Previously in 1796 and in 1805, three hundred horses had been evacuated from the stud, all the way to Hungary, to protect them from Napoleon's riders' depradations.

## The Cadre Noir in Saumur

**1** Duplessis-Mornay (1549 – 1623), author and French statesman, friend of Henri IV, was one of the most eminent members of the protestant party in the late sixteenth century.

**2** General Pierre Durand, (2008), *Mon équitation de cœur et de raison [My riding through heart and mind]*, Actes Sud.

**3** Head rider from 1919 – 1929.

**4** Future head rider, from 1935 – 1941.

**5** Head rider from 1825 – 1834.

**6** Head rider from 1847 – 1857.

**7** 1968 if one takes the Institut National d'Équitation (National Equestrian Institute) into account.

**8** From 1984 – 1996.

**9** From 1984 – 2006.

**10** Since 2002.

**11** Since 2002.

**12** Since 2008.

**13** Since 1984.

**14** Head rider from 1864 – 1872.

**15** General Blacque-Belair, head rider from 1909 – 1914.

**16** Head rider from 1999 – 2006.

## The Royal Andalusian School of Equestrian Art in Jerez

1 Michel Henriquet.

2 Under the command of head rider Colonel de Saint-André.

3 The tack room is air conditioned so that the leathers of the School's saddles, bridles and harness may remain supple.

## The Portuguese School of Equestrian Art in Lisbon

1 Which etymologically means "Royal Manège" and describes the equestrian exercises such as they were practised in Portugal in the eighteenth century.

2 Louis Fabre, (December 1985), *L'École portugaise d'art équestre [The Portuguese school of equestrian art]*, in: Plaisirs Équestres.

3 And, more precisely, the stud department of the Ministry of Agriculture.

4 He is one of the founders of the School, a veterinarian and international dressage competitor.

5 Louis Fabre, as before.

## The airs above the ground

1 Jean-Claude Barry, (2005), *Traité des airs relevés [Treatise on the airs above the ground]*, Belin.

2 *Ibidem.*

3 See definitions in the glossary.

4 See definitions in the glossary.

## The subtlety of art through schooling

1 If one considers that the show *How Andalusian horses dance* as well as the *doma vaquera* re-adopt some or all of the *Vueltas escaramuzas a la gineta* as they were presented in the heart of Jerez at the time.

2 Jean Lagoutte, (2007, 24 November), *Les quatre écoles : la recherche d'une esthétique atemporelle [The four schools: the search for a timeless aesthetic]* , contribution to the 11th symposium of the ENE, *Les Quatre Écoles d'art équestre, Vienne, Saumur, Lisbonne, Jerez patrimoine européen du XXIe siècle [The Four Schools of Equestrian Art, Vienna, Saumur, Lisbon, Jerez, 21st century European heritage]*, Bibliothèque Nationale de France.

3 Doctor of social sciences, riding instructor, German translator of the works of M.C. de Andrade, of General Faverot de Kerbrecht and Jean-Claude Racinet. In *La Guérinière "classique" chez Manuel Carlos de Andrade et Ludwig von Hünersdorf : aperçus sur l'histoire de la communauté et des divergences des équitations d'écoles des grandes écoles ["Classical" La Guérinière in Manuel Carlos de Andrade and Ludwig von Hünersdorf: insights into the history of the community and of the divergence of the school equitations of the great schools]*, contribution to the 11th symposium of the ENE, *Les Quatre Écoles d'art équestre, Vienne, Saumur, Lisbonne, Jerez patrimoine européen du XXIe siècle [The Four Schools of Equestrian Art, Vienna, Saumur, Lisbon, Jerez, 21st century European heritage]*, Bibliothèque Nationale de France, (2007, 24 November).

4 *Directives pour la conduite méthodique du dressage du cavalier et du cheval à l'École espagnole de Vienne [Directives for the methodical handling of the dressage of rider and horse at the Spanish Riding School in Vienna]*, (1898).

5 Louis Fabre, (2007, 24 November), *Les spécificités de l'équitation portugaise de Carlos d'Andrade à l'École portugaise d'art équestre [The characteristics of Carlos d'Andrade's Portuguese equitation at the Portuguese School of Equestrian Art]*, contribution to the 11th symposium of the ENE, *Les Quatre Écoles d'art équestre, Vienne, Saumur, Lisbonne, Jerez patrimoine européen du XXIe siècle [The Four Schools of Equestrian Art, Vienna, Saumur, Lisbon, Jerez, 21st century European heritage]*, Bibliothèque Nationale de France.

6 Author of *Luz da liberal e Nobre Arte da Cavallaria [Illustration of the free and noble art of horsemanship]*, published in 1790.

7 Jean-Pierre Tuloup, (2000), *Une histoire des écuyers du Cadre noir [A history of the Cadre Noir riders]*, Grandvaux.

8 Jean Lagoutte, as before.

9 The Duke of Newcastle.

## Glossary

1 Albert Decarpentry (French master rider, 1878 – 1956), *Équitation académique [Academic equitation]*, Lavauzelle.

2 The Duke of Newcastle.